GENOCIDE AND SOCIAL JUSTICE IN WESTERN AND EASTERN SOCIETY

Dr. Akram Muhammad and
Mrs. Nuzhat Alam Akram

Dedication

To my late parents, Father Major M. Mustafa (Retired Indian Army Officer) and Mother Mrs. Kulsoom Begum, who planted the seed of knowledge in my mind and nurtured it. They taught me that *"words have the power to change the world."*

Greatly loved and deeply missed are the sources of inspiration, guidance, and support: my late brother, Dr. M. Mukarram, Ph.D. (AMU), my late father-in-law CMO Dr. M. Shoeb Alam Khan, MBBS, MD, and my late sister Mrs. Nasimun Nisa Farhat, B.A., B.Ed. (AMU), M.A. (BHU).

Acknowledgment

We, Prof. Dr. Akram Mohammad, Ph.D. (Chem.), LL.M., and Hajjin Mrs. Nuzhat Alam Akram, B.A., Ph.A. (Canada), are extremely grateful to their family for encouraging us in all our pursuits and inspiring us to follow our dreams. We are thankful to our children, daughters, and sons for supporting us emotionally and financially, making it possible to complete this book. I am grateful to our wonderful family: wife, Mrs. Nuzhat Alam Akram, B.A., Ph.A. (Ottawa); our daughters, Miss Afreenish Yusirah Akram, B.Sc. Food Science, M.A. (Carleton University, Ottawa), Miss Parihan Israh Akram, B.Sc. Health Science (Carleton University, Ottawa), Miss Afrah Inshirah Akram, Grade 6; and my sons, Azfar Al-Affan Akram, B.Sc. Biotechnology, M.Sc. (University of Ottawa), Yawar Az-Farhan Akram, B.Sc. Biotechnology (University of Ottawa), Zafar Eshan Akram, B.Sc. Neuroscience (Carleton University, Ottawa), and Uzair Ziad Akram, B.Sc. (Carleton University, Ottawa).

Our extended gratitude to family in India, including my brothers: Col. Dr. M. Azam, M.D., Ph.D.; Prof. Dr. Muhazzim, M. Tech., Ph.D.; Prof. Dr. M. Aslam-Hameshgul, M.D.; Advocate Farhat Ashfaque, LL.B.; Principal M. Samiullah, M. Com; Capt. Sabir, Md. Ibrar. Gratitude to my mother-in-law, Mrs. Najma Khatoon; my sisters-in-law, Mrs. Rafat Alam, B.Sc., B.Ed., and Mrs. Farhat Alam, B.Tech., MBA; and my brother-in-law, Intekhab Alam.

A special thanks to my late father, Major M. Mustafa; my late mother, Mrs. Kulsoom Begum; my late brother, Dr. M. Mukarram; my late sisters, Mrs. Nasimun Nisa Farhat, Shabnam

Mustafa, and Razia Mustafa; my late father-in-law, CMO Dr. M. Shoeb Alam Khan; and family relatives, Late Mohd. Osama Alam, late Rustam Ali. Thanks to all my friends, family, relatives, and teachers for continuously inspiring and providing me with moral support to fulfill my dreams:

Thanks to my teachers: Prof. Firoz Ahmed (AMU), Dr. Omkar Nath Tripathi (CDRI), Dr. Abdul Mujeeb Kidwai (ITRC), Prof. B.B. Pande (LU), Dr. Rick Moody, Dr. Saeed Qureshi, the late Dr. Hari Vijay (Health Canada), Prof. Edward Lai (Carleton University), the late Prof. Jack Carnet, Prof. Ian Clark, Prof. Liam, Prof. James Gomes, Prof. Ajoy Basak, Prof. Mad Karen (University of Ottawa), Dr. Max Arela (Montreal University), the late Prof. Tahir Hussain (St. John university), Dr. Raphael Galea (NRC), Ms. Carrie Lynn Barkley, Lawyer (ACA, Ottawa), Dr. Hershal H.B. Kegan, and Dr. Serdal Sevinc.

Thanks to Prof. Abdus Salam, Nobel Prize winner in 1979, with whom I met and shook hands in 1981, near Sir Syed's grave and Jama Masque AMU, Aligarh, and learned how to accept and complete the hardest challenges in life first.

Thanks to my wife, Mrs. Nuzhat Alam Akram, for her financial support.

Finally, I am grateful to the book project team members for helping me complete this book.

About the Author

Prof. Dr. Akram Mohammad, Ph.D. (Chem.), LL.M., and Mrs. Nuzhat Alam Akram, B.A., Ph.A. (Canada) are the authors of the book "Genocide and Social Justice in Western and Eastern Society" Dr. Akram earned his Ph.D. in Chemistry from Aligarh Muslim University, India, and an LL.M. from Lucknow University, India. He also holds an M.Sc. in Accelerator Mass Spectrometry (AMS) from the University of Ottawa, Canada. He completed a postgraduate diploma in Regulatory Affairs from AAPS, Toronto, and a Paralegal certification from ACA, Ottawa. Dr. Akram conducted his M.Phil. and Ph.D. research at the Central Drug Research Institute (CDRI) in Lucknow and served as a Research Associate at the Industrial Toxicology Research Centre (ITRC), also in Lucknow. He received fellowships from the Council of Scientific and Industrial Research (CSIR) and the Indian Council of

Medical Research (ICMR). His LL.M. thesis focused on Crime Against Women, and he served as President of the Research Scientist and Fellow Association (RSFA) in Lucknow. He was also an Advocate and member of the Delhi Bar Council, India, and founded the Micro Library with Micro Funding initiative in India to support humanity and society. Dr. Akram worked as a Scientist for the FAO of the United Nations in the Ministry of Agriculture and Water Research Lab-NAWRC, Riyadh, Saudi Arabia, where he performed Hajj and Umrah in Makkah and Madinah. He was a Professor, Chairman, and Head of the Examination Board at the College of Pharmacy, Qassim University, Saudi Arabia.

In Canada, Dr. Akram was a Scientific Researcher at Health Canada, where he discovered and developed the Flow Through Diffusion Cell, a device to measure toxic chemicals in human skin. He also served as a Research and Teaching Associate at Carleton University, the National Research Council (NRC), and the University of Ottawa. Born in an army hospital in Madras, India, Dr. Akram grew up in Jamuwaon, Bilthraroad, Ballia, and Khairaty, Sivan-Chapra, Bihar. He received his education at Aligarh Muslim University, Lucknow University, and the University of Ottawa.

Dr. Akram's late father, Major M. Mustafa, was an Indian Army officer, and his late mother, Mrs. Kulsoom Begum, managed the family. He has four brothers (Col. Dr. Azam, Dr. Muazzam, late Dr. Mukarram, and Prof. Aslam) and three sisters (Mrs. Nasimun Nisa Farhat, late Miss Shabnam Mustafa, and late Miss Razia Mustafa). Dr. Akram married Nuzhat Alam, daughter of Dr. M. Shoeb Alam and Mrs. Najma Khatoon of Baheri, Ballia. They have three daughters (Afreenish, Parihan, and Afrah) and four sons (Azfar, Yawar, Zafar, and Uzair). The family currently resides in Nepean, Ottawa, Ontario, Canada.

Hajjin Mrs. Nuzhat Alam Akram is from Baheri, Ballia, and was born in Kanpur. She graduated from Baba Raghav Das Degree College, Devaria, Gorakhpur University. She attended her primary, middle, and high school at Kasturba Girls Inter College, Devaria, U.P. Her father, Dr. M. Shoeb Alam Khan, was CMO in Philiphit District, UP, Medical Department, and her mother, Mrs. Najma Khatoon, is a home manager. She has two sisters (Rafat and Farhat) and one brother (Intekhab). After graduation, she married Dr. Akram Mohammad and went to Saudi Arabia to perform Hajj and Umrah. Then she came to Ottawa, Canada, to study Pharmacy Assistant (Ph. A.). She has three daughters (Afreenish, Parihan, and Afrah) and four sons (Azfar, Yawar, Zafar, and Uzair). They can be reached via email at mnakram100@gmail.com

Preface

Human history has been full of violent accounts stemming from the killing instinct of man. From homicides to wars, the crimes humanity has inflicted upon its own kind is a horrific tale that repeats itself. However, the crime of genocide stands apart in its chilling purpose — the complete eradication of a group of people based on their ethnicity, race, religion, or nationality. The scale of the killing that occurs in genocides, as well as the cold-blooded intent behind it to wipe a group from the fabric of existence, makes this crime far more horrific than any other that mankind has been responsible for.

The Holocaust, Darfur, Rwanda, Bosnia, and Palestine all echo the blood-soaked tales of the genocide victims and the very few survivors who still fear the repetition of the mass atrocity they experienced in the past. However, these tales are buried with the victims as genocide has become a topic not many wish to speak on due to the horrors of man's cruelty that they would have to address and acknowledge.

The intent of writing this book is to explore the topic of genocide, which is often not discussed or, in some cases, even denied when brought up in conversation. As a result, confusion persists regarding the term and the crime it denotes. Compiling the available literature on genocide and its history, we intend to educate readers by providing them with a neutral, unbiased perspective on genocides that have occurred so far and the cruel impacts they have had on both Eastern and Western societies.

To evolve as a global community striving for peace and prosperity, we must address our existing conflicts, educate ourselves on their intent, and come together to bring a positive difference. This book also intends to spark intellectual debate on the preventive measures for genocide. Coming together to look for solutions rather than blaming the other is the way forward and the first initiative we should take to embrace a better and safer world.

While you are reading 'Genocide and Social Justice in Western and Eastern Society,' ponder on the reasons why these horrific crimes occurred and what steps we can take to curtail them. Equipped with a thorough knowledge of genocide and its impacts through this book, you can also decide where humanity stands in the present and whether the phrase 'Never Again' can truly ever reach fulfillment.

Contents

Chapter 1: Genocide

"You will be judged in years to come by how you responded to genocide on your watch."

- Nicholas Kristof

Genocide is a term that has been used increasingly in the last year ever since the attack on 7 October 2023 that gave birth to one of the deadliest massacres of our time. From worldwide protests for stopping the genocide in Palestine to the demands for a ceasefire in the U.N. and other international bodies, this term has become part of our daily conversation due to ongoing political affairs in the world.

However, what is genocide actually, and what can be its causes? What is the impact of genocide on society and the world, and why should we put an end to it?

Theoretically, genocide is the worst crime a group of people, authority, or government can commit against another race or group. Wiping out an entire race or nation through severe oppression and mass killing falls into the crimes of genocide.

However, most people are unfamiliar with this term and the extent of the horrors used to describe it. This book aims to delve deep into genocide's meaning, origin, and implementation. From historical examples, the case of genocide as a punishable offense and the need to stop it in these advancing times is discussed throughout this book.

What Is Genocide?

"You have to understand what caused genocide to happen. Or it will happen again."

- Tim Walz

Genocide is defined as the deliberate and systematic destruction of a group of people because of their ethnicity, nationality, religion, or race.[1] It is derived from the Greek words "*genos*," which means race, and "*cides*," which means to kill.

This term was coined in 1944 by Raphael Lemkin, a Polish-Jew lawyer, during the Second World War. Lemkin fled Nazi-occupied Poland in 1941 and gave the term Genocide to describe the heinous crimes that the Nazis were committing to oppress the Jews.

He first used this term in his book *Axis Rule in Occupied Europe*, originally published in 1944. Through this term, he intended for these crimes of mass killing, torture, and displacement to be recognized and punished by the international courts.

The Nuremberg Trials in 1945 marked the first case of persecution upon genocide.[2] After the Second World War, Nazi officials were tired and indicted for crimes against humanity. These trials continued for nine months and revealed all the war crimes committed against the Jews, becoming the first globally

---

[1] Genocide. (n.d.). Encyclopædia Britannica. https://www.britannica.com/topic/genocide
[2] Bamford, T. (2020). The Nuremberg Trial and its Legacy. The National WWII Museum | New Orleans. https://www.nationalww2museum.org/war/articles/the-nuremberg-trial-and-its-legacy

recognized case of Genocide that was addressed and punished. About twenty-four high-ranking leaders of the Nazis were penalized by the International Military Tribunal presiding over the case. As a result, in 1946, the U.N. General Assembly passed a resolution that labeled Genocide as a punishable offense.

Genocide includes the intentional targeting and killing of members of a specific racial or ethnic group, causing severe bodily or mental harm and deliberately subjecting the people to unlivable conditions that cause damage to them collectively. Imposing measures intended to prevent births within the group, forcibly transferring children, and displacing the people from their native lands is also a part of genocide.

Difference Between Genocide and Suicide

The term genocide may sound similar to suicide, but there is a distinct difference between the two. Genocide refers to mass killing or taking the life of a group of people or race, while suicide refers to taking one's own life.

Both the terms have the suffix *cide*, which means to kill, but the subject in question is different. Suicide means to deliberately take one's life due to hatred, self-loathing, or other mental issues.[3] In suicide, the individual's life is at risk of being terminated, while in genocide, multiple lives are at risk of being mercilessly wiped out.

---

[3] WHO EMRO | Suicide | Health topics. (n.d.). World Health Organization - Regional Office for the Eastern Mediterranean. https://www.emro.who.int/health-topics/suicide/feed/atom.html

An example that clearly defines the difference between these terms is the aftermath of the Second World War. The Nazis of the Third Reich committed genocide by attempting to wipe out the Jews. But when the war ended and the Nuremberg Trials were held in Bavaria, most of the prominent Nazi figures committed suicide to escape the trial and punishment. Adolf Hitler, the leader of the German Nazis Party and feared dictator, took his life on 30 April 1945 by shooting himself in the head. His act of ending his life was suicide. In contrast, the war crimes committed by the Nazis under his command are referred to as genocide.

Similarly, the term Homicide is used for the killing of one person by another.[4] An individual life is taken in this case, but it is different from suicide and genocide. Homicide is also a punishable offense, with the death penalty being the maximum sentence.

Genocide and Other War Crimes

"Genocide is not just a murderous madness; it is, more deeply, a politics that promises a utopia beyond politics - one people, one land, one truth, the end of difference. Since genocide is a form of political utopia, it remains an enduring temptation in any multiethnic and multicultural society in crisis."

- Michael Ignatieff

As humanity suffered throughout the years from war and oppression, various conventions were held to recognize the

---

[4] Homicide. (n.d.). Encyclopædia Britannica. https://www.britannica.com/topic/homicide

crimes that people should be protected from. The Genocide Convention is one of the earliest examples to prosecute genocide and other war crimes. In the 2005 United Nations World Summit, it was globally accepted by the member Heads of the States to protect their people from four types of crimes: genocide, war crimes, crimes against humanity, and ethnic cleansing.[5]

While we know now that genocide is the mass killing of a group of people, the other types of crimes that are highly detrimental to humanity and condemned as strongly are as follows:

War Crimes: The International Criminal Court (ICC) defines war crimes as the willful killing, torture, or inhuman treatment of people during wars. War crimes also include extensive damage to property that was not carried out as a part of military necessity. Violation of laws and customs (disrespecting the dead, violating religious places, attacking hospitals) are also included in seriously punishable war crimes. These crimes are considered severe breaches of the 1949 Genevan Convention that applies to all international armed conflicts.

Crimes against Humanity: Crimes against humanity is a vast domain that has not yet been included in a separate international law treaty. These crimes refer to acts of violence, murder, oppression, and prosecution that do not take place during wars. Crimes against humanity include extermination, murder, torture, mass displacement, deportation, sexual violence, and slavery. However, isolated or accidental acts of violence are not included

---

[5] Defining the Four Mass Atrocity Crimes. (2018). Global Centre for the Responsibility to Protect. https://www.globalr2p.org/publications/defining-the-four-mass-atrocity-crimes/

in this category. According to the Roman Statute of ICC, crimes against humanity are violent acts carried out on a large scale or in a broad geographical context.

Ethnic Cleansing: Ethnic cleansing is defined by the U.N. Commission of Experts as rendering an area ethnically homogeneous by using force or intimidation to remove persons of given groups from the area.[6] This term was used to define the conflicts in Yugoslavia that were targeting civilian groups and brutally wiping out their existence. Some other cases of ethnic cleansing include the Rohingya-Muslim conflict in Myanmar. Several experts state that the ongoing genocide in Palestine is also an example of ethnic cleansing as a specific group is forcefully displaced from their land and killed.

These crimes have been declared as the Four Mass Atrocity Acts by the International Criminal Court and are mentioned in the globally accepted 1949 Genevan Convention and The Genocide Convention. These acts cause severe damage to the core dignity and well-being of mankind in times of war or peace; therefore, they have been strictly condemned by the international courts and the United Nations.

Early Cases of Genocide

"What connects two thousand years of genocide? Too much power in too few hands."

- Simon Wiesenthal

---

[6] Ethnic Cleansing. (n.d.). Encyclopædia Britannica. https://www.britannica.com/topic/ethnic-cleansing

Although genocide is a relatively recent term, the crime has been committed since the advent of time. The root cause seems to be the superiority complex engrained in the human mind, as people wish to show themselves as superior and more powerful than others. Violence becomes a means for them to display their power and provoke fear in the hearts of their enemies. This mentality has been responsible for groups of humans fighting and killing each other from the very start of life on Earth.

The earliest reported case of genocide that was recognized by the world might be the Jewish Holocaust, but the killing instinct of humans has been responsible for wiping out other races long before the world wars.

Tribal conflicts in ancient times on land, hunting, and agriculture can be considered genocide as mass killings occurred. Later, religion and ethnicity became the basis of these conflicts as one superior group started to wipe out other weaker groups to assert their dominance.

Similarly, the wars and crusades of medieval times include massacres of entire villages and towns. Lastly, the destruction that plagued humanity during the First and Second World Wars was also a major genocide against the global population. The bombing of Hiroshima and Nagasaki, as well as the Jewish Holocaust, marked dark times in the history of the world as millions of people were killed, detonated, and displaced. However, the World Wars were not the first reported cases of genocide.

The mass destruction of the city of Carthage in 146 BCE is considered the first reported case of Genocide, according to Ben

Kiernan, an Australian-American Historian and founding Director of the Cambodian Genocide Program.[7] The Romans besieged Carthage and destroyed most of the city, while about 150,000 Carthaginians out of the total 2400,000 were killed. The first written record of the genocide at Carthage was found in Livy's volumes on the *History of Rome from its Foundation*, rediscovered and printed in 1531.

Recent Cases of Genocide

Over the past ten to fifteen years, acts of genocide have increased alarmingly and become more dangerous compared to the past. The vast options of biological and chemical warfare due to the advancement of science and technology put us at even more risk, as genocide is deadlier in the 21st Century, and millions of people can be wiped out singlehandedly.

The evolution of bombs from atom bombs to even deadlier hydrogen bombs presents a persistent threat of lethal chemical warfare. On the other hand, viruses such as COVID-19 are examples of biological warfare to eliminate a mass population from the world. These methods have made genocide easier and twice more dangerous than it was in the past, about a hundred years back.

Earlier, genocide was localized and confined only to a small geographical area, such as a city or a settlement. However, with the advancement of weapons, large areas can also be covered

[7] Kiernan, B. (2004). The First Genocide: Carthage, 146 BC. Diogenes, 3, 27–39. https://doi.org/10.1177/0392192104043648

without the restriction of geographical borders. Dangerous nuclear bombs and air strikes can wipe out entire countries.

Some of the recent cases of genocide are discussed below:

Bosnian Genocide: When the government of Bosnia-Herzegovina declared its independence from Yugoslavia in 1992, the Bosnian Serb leaders carried out a genocide of Bosniak (Bosnian Muslims) and Croatian civilians.[8] About 100,000 people were killed as a result, out of which about eighty percent of the martyrs were Bosniak. After the Nuremberg Trials, the Bosnian Genocide was the first international tribunal that resulted in prosecution based on genocide and the indictment of 161 people.

Rwandan Genocide: In 1994, the Tutsi minority in Rwanda was targeted by the Hutu ethnic majority, and about 800,000 people were murdered, mostly belonging to the minority.[9] This genocide forced people to pick weapons against their neighbors, resulting in a drastic humanitarian crisis as two million refugees fled Rwanda, and millions of people were killed by the time the situation was brought under control.

Palestinian Genocide: The most recent case is the ongoing genocide in Palestine, mainly in the West Bank and Gaza. Israel's continuous oppression and mass killing through bombs and air strikes have resulted in the Palestinian death toll crossing more than twenty-nine thousand people. Israel is forcibly cleansing

---

[8] Bosnian Genocide - Timeline, Cause & Herzegovina. (n.d.). HISTORY. https://www.history.com/topics/1990s/bosnian-genocide

[9] Rwandan Genocide - Facts, Response & Trials. (n.d.). HISTORY. https://www.history.com/topics/africa/rwandan-genocide

Gaza and the West Bank by displacing and killing the native Palestinians to claim the rightful land of Palestine as their own.

Possibility of a Muslim Genocide in India: Muslims form about fifteen percent of the total Indian population. However, they are constantly under threat of conflicts and mob lynching by extremist Hindus. With the introduction of the National Registration Record, the Muslim minorities would have to prove their identity as Indian, or else they would be expelled from the country as illegal Bengali immigrants.[10] Furthermore, the Citizenship Amendment Act passed in 2019 grants citizenship to persecuted minorities from India's neighboring countries, but Muslims are not included in those minorities, hinting at the government's Anti-Muslim political approach. These legal interventions may result in a future genocide, with the Indian Muslims being displaced to Bangladesh or otherwise tortured and killed.

Aside from these few cases, several accounts of genocide have taken place in recent times. The carpet bombing of Syria and Afghanistan, the displacement and torture of Rohingya Muslims in Myanmar, and the conflicts in Kashmir are all examples of genocide in the 21st Century.

---

[10] Sarwar, M. (2022). India's National Register of Citizens: A Tool for Muslim Disenfranchisement – Synergy: The Journal of Contemporary Asian Studies. Synergy: The Journal of Contemporary Asian Studies. https://utsynergyjournal.org/2022/01/17/indias-national-register-of-citizens-a-tool-for-muslim-disenfranchisement/

Effects of Genocide on the Society

Genocide has long-lasting effects on society and impacts the population adversely, as discussed below.

Refugees: The most common impact of genocide is the formation of refugees. Refugees are people who leave their homes or are forced to leave to seek safety or refuge.[11] After the genocide, the people who survived the mass killings are referred to as refugees, and they are left with no safe place or shelter to go to. Their identity is lost, and they do not have passports, legal documentation, and rights to move from one place to another, which makes them face harsh living conditions even after the genocide ends. Education, healthcare, and other fundamental civilian rights are denied to these people, and even though they were leaving their homes to escape violation of rights, their current conditions expose them to further violation of rights and violence.

Fear: After facing mass killings, displacement, and loss of family members, fear gets ingrained in the hearts of those people who managed to survive the genocide. They fear what the future might bring, and the constant anxiety of facing the same situation all over again stops them from moving on. Most people are so adversely affected that the trauma causes them to take their own lives. This fear and resentment created in the society shuns its growth and confines the people into an anxious bubble of living in a constant state of terror.

---

[11] McMorran, C. (2016). Refugees. Beyond Intractability. https://www.beyondintractability.org/essay/refugees

Dehumanization: Another effect of genocide is the dehumanization of people suffering from the killings and torture. From Hitler labeling the Jews as vermin and Hutus labeling the Tutsi as cockroaches, it diminishes the realization that human lives are at stake during the genocide. The weaker side is treated lowly, and it adversely impacts their self-esteem, causing humiliation and distress even after the end of the killings and torture.

Failing Economy: With most of the people targeted and killed, the economy suffers as there is less workforce, fewer resources, and more damage to counter. The costs of genocide in rebuilding infrastructure and redevelopment from scratch take a toll on the economy. People have to depend on humanitarian aid to survive; often, it is not enough to live properly. This failing economy impacts society as a whole and restricts people from returning to their everyday lives before the genocide occurred.

The global impact of genocide is devastating as it damages international relations between the countries in conflict, spreads trauma and fear in the worldwide community, and causes emotional burdens. The refugees created as a result of genocide spread to neighboring countries, causing strain on their resources as well.[12]

Genocide is an evil that causes extreme damage to the victimized groups as well as the global community. Due to the killing instinct of humans, genocide has existed from the earliest

---

[12] The Global Impact of Genocide. (2022). IvyPanda. https://ivypanda.com/essays/the-global-impact-of-genocide/

of times, but now, knowing all the repercussions of taking such extreme measures, we should put a stop to it.

This book discusses how you can play a role in stopping genocide, raising awareness, and taking the correct steps as a responsible human being for the betterment of humanity in general. The first step to stopping evil is to be aware of the extent and the consequences. Thus, this book is a minor effort to raise awareness so that people can choose wisely and put an end to the hatred that inevitably results in genocide.

Chapter 2: History of Genocide

"The most persistent sound which reverberates through man's history is the beating of war drums."

- Arthur Koestler

The term *Genocide* was coined in 1944, but the phenomenon itself is ancient, dating back to prehistoric times. Acts of human destructiveness have occurred throughout history; however, the causes for these acts vary with time. In the very beginning, humans were killed for survival, land, and resources. Eventually, these reasons expanded to include religious conflicts, ideological differences, and the assertion of power and dominion.

The timeline of genocide started from the early times and continues to this day due to man's unquenchable thirst for power. The recent cases of genocide in Gaza, Sudan, Rwanda, and Myanmar prove that even after all the technological advancement, the human instinct to kill and rule remains the same. In fact, it has only gotten deadlier with time as science and technology have enabled man to create more lethal weapons than earlier. Wars can be caused and end by pressing a single button, populations can be wiped out completely, and generations can be affected for the years to come. This concept of weapons of mass destruction nowadays has increased the horror of genocide.

Genocide in Prehistoric Times

In prehistoric times, the human population was limited, and the only priority back then was survival. Survival against wild animals, extreme temperatures, and disease caused man to live in groups in the Paleolithic period more than 15,000 years ago and earlier. Killings occurred in those times among groups as they fought for resources, land, and power. By the Mesolithic period, people had begun to domesticate animals and practice agriculture, so killing other groups meant seizing control of their land and animals, thus having more resources to feed and survive on. Another reason for genocide in the Stone Age was making human sacrifices to the gods for rain, expelling disease, removing curses, etc.

Skeletons dating back to the Stone Age found in Italy, Poland, Spain, and Egypt show skull injuries through blunt objects such as stones and other primitive tools used as weapons back then. Rock paintings discovered in the caves of southeastern Spain show wounded archers, battle scenes, and execution processions, indicating that genocide existed from the advent of human existence. Even in those times when man wasn't as advanced and had primitive knowledge of agriculture and war, the concept of killing other humans and destroying groups existed.[13]

[13] Danylchenko, K. (2023). Why people started killing each other. WAS. https://was.media/en/2023-03-09-why-people-started-killing-each-other/

Genocide in the Classical World

The Classical World is known for the Greek and Roman civilizations, which started a significant chapter in history. While the Greeks were responsible for introducing philosophy, democracy, and free thought into society, the Romans who succeeded them brought the idea of an Empire stretching far beyond their geographical boundaries. The earliest reported case of genocide in Carthage also dates to this period.

In 100 BCE, the Roman Republic faced civil wars and genocide until 44 BCE, with Julius Caesar becoming the first dictator. After his assassination, Octavian came to power and became the first Emperor of Rome, starting the glorious yet bloodthirsty era of Roman expansion.

The competition for resources, land, and power increased, and the weapons became comparatively more dangerous than the rocks, stones, and arrows used by the Stone Age people. With the introduction of bronze and iron to make weapons such as swords, spears, and shields, killing people became easier as these weapons helped eliminate with a single strike. The Romans were known for their advanced warfare techniques, such as the *testudo* (a protective formation for attacking fortresses) and the military bases like miniature cities with all the services necessary to support a legion.[14]

The Roman Empire came to an end with the last Emperor Romulus, in 476 BCE, but the world was plagued with wars, and

---

[14] Editors of Kingfisher. (2001). The Concise History Encyclopedia. Kingfisher.

mass killings carried out by the Barbarians, the Huns, and the Kushans in the Eurasian region.

Genocide in the Middle Ages

In the Middle Ages, cases of genocide became deadlier as the Roman Empire had set a standard for power, and the regions under their rule now transitioned into territories and countries ruled by kings. Warfare training became common, and genocide thrived in medieval times. Kings led their armies to war against other territories, resulting in the more powerful group wiping out the weaker ones. This is known as Institutionalized Genocide.[15]

Genocide became a tool for conquest in the Middle Ages. People who couldn't be governed through politics were killed. The Byzantines, Persians, Mongols, and other medieval groups expanded their empires through mass killing and fear.

The High Middle Ages (1050-1300 CE) are known for the Crusades, which gave rise to the first cases of Ideological Genocide. The religious basis of these Crusades and the involvement of the Roman Catholic Church in these wars show an ideology governing the causes behind the elimination of a particular group of people (in this case, those who were not Christians or refused to convert). The Last Crusade was fought in 1291 CE, and the Crusaders lost the war to the Muslims. The Mamluks gained power in Egypt, stopped the advances of Genghis Khan, and later captured Crusader cities after defeating the Europeans. It was also an example of Ideological Genocide as

---

[15] Smith, R. W. (2000). Genocide and the Modern Age (pp. 21–36). Syracuse University Press.

Muslims had religious influences behind their conquests, known as Jihaad.[16]

The Ottoman Empire extended its reign over much of Southeast Europe, West Asia, and North Africa between the 14th and early 20th centuries. The Mongols converted to Islam and settled in the subcontinent as the Mughals. However, genocide continued to occur in wars and conquests as different dynasties rose to power and fought for geographical and political control.

Genocide of Native Americans

The Spanish Conquistadores in the 16th Century laid the foundation for a series of genocides that would take place on American soil. The Spaniards invaded Central and South America, destroying the Aztec and Inca Empires. It was the first case of Genocide by European settlers who came to the Americas. However, it was just the beginning of the gradual elimination of Native Americans that continued up to the late 19th Century.[17]

North America also faced a similar fate in the 1600s as European settlers came hungry for land and destroyed the native settlements. Villages were wiped out, and the Native Americans were forcefully driven out of their homelands while the settlers continued to colonize America. The killing and expulsion of Native Americans can be referred to as genocide due to the nature of the crimes committed against them. The settlers did not consider the Natives to be humans like themselves. Instead,

---

[16] Aslan, R. (2010). The Crusades: Definition, Religious Wars & Facts. HISTORY. https://www.history.com/topics/middle-ages/crusades#effects-of-the-crusades
[17] Editors of Kingfisher. (2001). The Concise History Encyclopedia. Kingfisher.

they were denied the right to exist. Whether they cooperated with the settlers or not, they were mistreated and referred to as alien others, as intellectually and physically deficient. Therefore, genocide that occurred with the Native Americans was both institutionalized and utilitarian as settlers took their land and resources, forcing them to live as refugees in their own homeland.[18]

The Gnadenhutten Massacre in 1782, the Battle of Tippecanoe in the early 1800s, the Creek War, also known as the Red Stick War, the Mankato Executions, and the Sand Creek Massacres all resulted in heavy losses of Native American lives. By the late 19th Century, less than 238,000 Indigenous people of North America remained of the estimated 5 million population before European settlements.[19]

World War I

After the Roman Empire, the Crusades, the Ottoman Empire, and the European Settlement in America, the most notable cases of genocide and mass destruction were the World Wars. What started as an assassination of Archduke Franz Ferdinand, the heir to the Austro-Hungarian throne, gained traction and resulted in World War I. Austria-Hungary, backed up by Germany, declared war on Serbia, which was allied with Russia and France. Thus, the

---

[18] Abdoo, J. A. (1992). The Scourge of "Discovery": A Case Study of the Genocide of Native Americans in English North America . Dissertations, Theses, and Masters Projects, William & Mary College of Arts and Sciences. https://doi.org/https://dx.doi.org/doi:10.21220/s2-fjh6-8f64

[19] Fixico, D. L. (2018). When Native Americans Were Slaughtered in the Name of 'Civilization.' HISTORY. https://www.history.com/news/native-americans-genocide-united-states

European powers were roped into the war as their allies were being threatened.[20]

However, several historians chart the causes of World War I to date back to events prior to the assassination, such as the Russo-Japanese War in 1904-5, the annexation of Bosnia and Herzegovina by Austria-Hungary in 1908, the Second Moroccan Crisis in 1911, and the Balkan wars in 1912-13. All these events served as the rising conflicts that drove the world to war.

The total civilian and military casualties in World War I are recorded to be 40 million. About 14% of combat troops and six thousand soldiers were killed per day during the war that lasted from 1914 to 1918.[21] The League of Nations was founded after the First World War ended to avoid such a mass level of killings and destruction. However, it failed to prevent the Second World War, which broke out in the 1940s.

World War II and the Holocaust

The world had not yet fully recovered from the aftermath of the First World War when World War II broke out. It involved more than fifty nations and was one of the deadliest wars ever fought due to the advancement of weapons, such as the creation of missiles and atom bombs. Therefore, World War II's casualty rate was higher than World War I's. By the end of World War II, about 60 to 80 million people had been subjected to death. Out

---

[20] Kiger, P. J. (2021). 8 Events that Led to World War I. HISTORY. https://www.history.com/news/world-war-i-causes

[21] Mougel, N. (2011). World War I casualties. REPERES. https://www.census.gov/history/pdf/reperes112018.pdf

of these casualties, six million people were the Jews killed in the Nazi concentration camps.[22]

Hitler was elected the Chancellor of Germany in 1933 and started to mobilize the German military forces, violating the Treaty of Versailles that had been signed after the First World War. In 1938, Hitler sent troops to occupy Austria, and shortly after, he annexed Czechoslovakia. However, his military attempts went unchecked by France and Britain, who were recovering from the devastating aftermath of World War I. The temporary silence on their part emboldened the Nazis to take a step further, and Hitler signed the German-Soviet Non-Aggression Pact. This pact stirred trouble for France and Britain as Germany had Soviet support.

In 1939, Nazi Germany invaded Poland, a state to which France and Britain had promised military support. Thus, the European powers came to the aid of their ally and declared war on Germany. By then, Nazi troops had been militarized and were prepared to counter and attack ruthlessly. As a result, another global war started, which caused notably more destruction than the first one due to the advancement of chemical and mobile warfare.

The Holocaust, which took place during the Second World War, marks a dark time in the history of humanity. It was the event that eventually led to the coining of the term Genocide (killing of race) by Polish Jew Raphael Lemkin in 1944. Hitler's *Final Solution* of eliminating all European Jews marked one of the

---

[22] World War II: Summary, Combatants & Facts. (2009). HISTORY. https://www.history.com/topics/world-war-ii/world-war-ii-history

deadliest genocides as more than six million people fell prey to the Nazi concentration camps. They were treated as vermin and eliminated painfully. The concentration camp at Auschwitz, preserved to this day, narrates the horrifying tale of cruelty and mass murder of the Jews initiated by the Nazis.[23]

Furthermore, the atomic bombs dropped on Hiroshima and Nagasaki were another example of genocide that destroyed not only the people living in the cities at that time but also their future generations. Nuclear bombs cause extreme destruction, wiping out entire populations and crippling their generations for years to come. Japan suffered drastically from these bombings, and about 135,000 casualties occurred in Hiroshima, while 65,000 people were killed in Nagasaki.[24]

Genocide 1946 – 1999

The twentieth century was dubbed the *Age of Genocide* by Albert Camus, as both World Wars took place, but even after all that horror and destruction, genocides continued to occur over time. The Bosnian Genocide and Rwandan Genocide are a few of the cases in which mass killings occurred, and their oppressors wiped out a particular racial or ethnic group.

In the timeline of genocide, another tragic chapter is marked by the Nakba of 1948. Thousands of indigenous Palestinians were

---

[23] Genocide Timeline. (n.d.). Holocaust Encyclopedia | United States Holocaust Memorial Museum. Retrieved February 29, 2024, from https://encyclopedia.ushmm.org/content/en/article/genocide-timeline

[24] Total Casualties | The Atomic Bombings of Hiroshima and Nagasaki. (n.d.). Atomicarchive.Com: Exploring the History, Science, and Consequences of the Atomic Bomb. https://www.atomicarchive.com/resources/documents/med/med_chp10.html

driven out of their homes and massacred in the name of establishing a Jewish state in Palestine. It is both an example of genocide and ethnic cleansing, not long after the Holocaust that occurred in the Second World War. Approximately 75% of Palestinians were expelled from their homes, while the Israeli militia systematically destroyed more than 400 Palestinian cities and towns.[25]

Communist China in 1949 went through a cultural revolution brought upon by Mao Zedong, who established the People's Republic of China. During the Great Leap Forward, a five-year economic plan by Mao Zedong and the Chinese Communist Party, about 35 to 45 million Chinese were killed due to mass starvation, executions, and famine.[26]

Genocides after 2000

The Twenty-first Century is known for the rise of terrorism with the bombing of the Pentagon and the World Trade Center, which is remembered as 9/11. Although it was a systematic act of destruction and almost three thousand people were killed in the aftermath, there is debate on whether to consider it genocide or not. It has been referred to as genocidal terrorism by several scholars. However, the main difference between terrorism and genocide is that terrorism aims to spread terror through violent

---

[25] Quick Facts: The Palestinian Nakba ("Catastrophe"). (2023). Institute for Middle East Understanding (IMEU). https://imeu.org/article/quick-facts-the-palestinian-nakba

[26] The Investopedia Team. (2012). Great Leap Forward: What It Was, Goals, and Impact. Investopedia; Investopedia. https://www.investopedia.com/terms/g/great-leap-forward.asp#toc-what-is-the-great-leap-forward

acts, while genocide is the eradication of a particular group through violence.[27]

The Darfur Genocide took place in Western Sudan, becoming the first genocide of the Twenty-first Century. Since February 2003, government-sponsored militias eradicated the Darfuris, with about 400,000 people dying from violence, starvation, and disease. It is estimated that more than 2.8 million people were displaced in this genocide.[28]

In the Rakhine state of northwestern Myanmar, the Rohingya Muslims were subjected to genocide and driven out of the country. More than 3000 people were killed, with about 270,000 displaced from their homeland. Even today, the Muslim minority living in Myanmar fears persecution.[29] Most of the Rohingya refugees now live in camps in Bangladesh, unable to return to their country. The International Court of Justice accused Myanmar of committing genocide against the Rohingyas in 2019. However, the government denied all allegations.[30]

The most recent case of genocide after the 2000s is the ongoing genocide in Palestine. The Israeli government and military forces continue to starve and kill the population of Gaza and the West Bank under the guise of eliminating Hamas. Using

---

[27] Zimmerer, J. (2006). From the Editors: genocidal terrorism? A plea for conceptual clarity. Journal of Genocide Research, 4, 379–381. https://doi.org/10.1080/14623520601086122

[28] Modern Era Genocides. (n.d.). Genocide Education Project. Retrieved March 1, 2024, from https://genocideeducation.org/resources/modern-era-genocides/

[29] Rohingya. (n.d.). Human Rights Watch | Defending Human Rights Worldwide. https://www.hrw.org/tag/rohingya

[30] European nations join Myanmar genocide case | Genocide News (2023). Al Jazeera. https://www.aljazeera.com/news/2023/11/17/five-european-nations-join-myanmar-genocide-case

white phosphorus, air strikes, and missiles to destroy the Palestinians while refusing access to humanitarian aid has resulted in more than thirty thousand deaths so far, and the majority of Palestinian cities have been reduced to rubble. It has so far been the most controversial and deadliest genocide of modern times, with millions protesting against it, yet no strict action has been taken to stop it.[31]

"The history of man is the history of crimes, and history can repeat. So, information is a defense. Through this, we can build, we must build, a defense against repetition."

- Simon Wiesenthal

The timeline of genocide existed even before the term was introduced to name the crime of mass killing of a particular race or group of humans. Raphael Lemkin describes genocide as the intentional infliction of mass destruction upon a specific group, race, or nation under cover of war, calling it a threat to international peace. However, years after its condemnation, the Genocide Convention, and the resolutions passed by the International Court of Justice, this heinous act continues to take place. The history of genocide has repeated itself several times as perhaps we fail to learn about the repercussions of causing such mass human destruction from our past.

[31] Lakhani, N. (2024). Israel is deliberately starving Palestinians, UN rights expert says | Israel-Gaza war. The Guardian. https://www.theguardian.com/world/2024/feb/27/un-israel-food-starvation-palestinians-war-crime-genocide

Chapter 3: Human Instinct

"The strongest human instinct is self-preservation."

- Iris Watts

From the very beginning, humans have existed based on their instincts. By instinct, man is a predator, a hunter, and a fighter. At first, these instincts were focused on survival against the extreme weather, wild animals, and other challenges of the undeveloped world. Then, as the cave-dwellers and hunter-gatherers transitioned into village-dwelling farmers who used tools for hunting and agriculture, self-preservation became a killing instinct. Humans became focused on protecting what was theirs and taking what belonged to others by force.[32]

According to Daly and Wilson, authors of the book *Homicide,* murderous intentions in humans stem as a by-product of urges towards some other goal. Self-preservation can be one of those reasons, but history provides a detailed account of territory, social standing, sexuality, and assertion of dominance as the main reasons behind the violent acts of murder committed by humans. From the early tribal people who killed other groups to seize control of their livestock and women to the conquests in the Classical World and Middle Ages to strengthen empires, humans have taken part in both homicide and genocide, fueled by a killing instinct.[33]

---

[32] Editors of Kingfisher. (2001). The Concise History Encyclopedia. Kingfisher.
[33] Jones, D. (2008). Human Behavior: Killer instincts. Nature, 7178, 512–515. https://doi.org/10.1038/451512a

Killing—A Human Instinct

"A sword never kills; it is a tool in the killer's hand."

- ***Lucius Annaeus Seneca***

The story of Cain and Abel, the sons of Adam, denotes one of the earliest recorded instances of homicide due to the killing instinct in humans. Jealousy and rivalry became the prime reasons behind Cain's decision to kill his brother, marking the first homicide in human history, according to both the Bible and the Holy Quran. History depicts various cases in which humans have killed their kind in wars, conflicts, oppression, and genocide. However, the question remains whether the killer instinct was naturally a part of our genes or acquired over time, as suggested by evolutionary psychology. A thorough debate exists on the topic, backed up by science and psychology, to prove that violence is a part of our psychological and genetic makeup, influencing the way we behave with other humans when led to aggression.

Humans tend to be more violent than other animals, as they are social and territorial creatures. Research conducted on 1,024 species of mammals, including 600 different human populations dating back to the Stone Age, shows that other members of the same species cause 0.3 percent of all deaths on average for all mammals. However, the rate of violence in humans is about seven times higher, comparatively similar to other primates like chimpanzees and apes. Similarities were also found in the way humans kill or get rid of a group and the coalition of chimpanzees to attack other groups, suggesting that primates tend to be more territorial and aggressive due to their genetics and lifestyle.[34]

To explain the neurobiology behind the connection between murders and psychology, a study carried out in 1997 by Adrian Raine, Lori LaCasse, and Monte Buchsbaum proves that people who are more violent experience more mental activity in the limbic system that drives aggression. The brains of forty-one murderers who had claimed guilty of murder (not by insanity) were studied, showing the same results. The prefrontal cortex, responsible for subduing the violent thoughts circulating in the brain, did not function as well as it does in non-violent people, making them unable to control their emotions and eventually giving into aggression and violent means. Thus, the killing instinct might have genetic, psychological, and neurobiological roots in humans.[35]

The *Homicide Adaptation Theory* proposed by David Buss and Joshua Duntley states that humans have committed homicide where the costs of killing members of their kind were less than the benefits achieved by their elimination. These benefits could be reducing the burden on the group by eliminating the sick or elderly, killing an unwanted child, eliminating competition by getting rid of a rival, gaining access to a competitor's resources,

---

[34] Fields, R. D. (2016). Humans Are Genetically Predisposed to Kill Each Other. Psychology Today. https://www.psychologytoday.com/us/blog/the-new-brain/201610/humans-are-genetically-predisposed-kill-each-other

[35] Jones, D. (2008). Human Behavior: Killer instincts. Nature, 7178, 512–515. https://doi.org/10.1038/451512a

protecting one's resources, territory, shelter, and food, asserting dominance, etc.[36]

Thus, the killing instinct has prevailed in humans from the very beginning when they lived in caves and continues to modern times when wars and moral conflicts further complicate the reasons behind the coordinated elimination of members of the same species.

Genocide Resulting from Human Instinct

Understanding how the killing instinct led to homicide is fundamental to understanding the reasons behind genocide. It is the mass killing of people based on ethnicity, race, or religion that makes them part of the *other* group. It is a continuation of groups or tribes of prehistoric humans fighting and killing other tribes to assert their dominance. The methods, weapons, and strategies have changed over time, but the act of killing remains the same, and so do the reasons.

A common factor behind genocide is the *'Us Against Them'* mentality. Believing that one group was superior to others, hence it had the right to eliminate the weaker group, gave birth to the concept of genocide. From the landlords killing their slaves for not completing their tasks on time to the kings punishing the masses for revolting against them, genocide has occurred in different forms throughout history. Often, it has been cloaked in the garb of war and terrorism, but the foundations remain

---

[36] Duntley, J. D., & Buss, D. M. (2011). Homicide adaptations. Aggression and Violent Behavior, 5, 399–410. https://doi.org/10.1016/j.avb.2011.04.016

unchanged. There is always a more substantial group oppressing the weak, ultimately leading to their elimination.

The *'Us Against Them'* mentality has deepened further in human minds due to patriotism and nationalism. Love for one's country or homeland can easily be used to turn them against other countries by infusing the need to protect their country from enemy attacks. Similarly, religious groups can turn against each other and propagate violence by urging the people to fight and kill in the name of God. Social groups, races, and ethnicities can use a similar approach to stress the need to kill *others* to ensure their survival and dominance. This mentality is extremely dangerous as it can lead humans to war against their kind, causing immeasurable death and destruction.[37]

Almost all the genocides that have taken place in history or are current at the moment have risen from this mentality in which one group is classified as weak, making others believe that it will be okay to terminate them as they do not deserve to live. It is a twisted implementation of Darwin's *Theory of Evolution* (Survival of the Fittest) in which a strong group considers itself the decider of the other group's fate, driving it out of their homeland or subjected it to mass killing because, according to them, the weaker group didn't deserve or wasn't fit enough to survive. The Native Americans were killed and driven out of their homes based on the same ideology. The United States stands witness to another case of racial segregation and apartheid based on color, subjecting the African American population to

---

[37] "Us Against Them" Mentality: Why Is It Dangerous? (2024). WebMD. https://www.webmd.com/mental-health/what-is-the-us-against-them-mentality

tortuous living conditions and massacre. The Hindu-Muslim conflicts in India are fueled by the *Us Against Them* mentality, and the Jewish Holocaust can also be linked to similar roots.

Israel-Palestine Conflict

The Israel-Palestine conflict is the result of ongoing aggression and violence between two groups. Both sides have suffered heavy losses over the years, but there seems no possible end to the conflict now or in the future. The death toll in Gaza and the West Bank continues to rise as Palestinians are being bombed by Israeli militants. It is probably the most prolonged ongoing conflict and genocide in world history, with roots dating back to the early 20th Century. A series of events leading to the attack on 7th October 2023 is said to have fueled the Israel-Gaza War that has resulted in more than thirty thousand Palestinian deaths so far. To understand the root of the conflict, all those events from the history of this conflict have to be addressed.

Fall of the Ottoman Empire: The Ottoman Empire started declining in the 1700s, losing most of its states to European powers. By the end of the First World War, it had been dissolved, and the region of Palestine and modern-day Israel came under Britain's rule following a League of Nations mandate. By then, the area held a majority of Arabs and a slowly increasing population of Jews.[38]

The Balfour Declaration: In 1917, the Balfour Declaration was signed, promising to create a Jewish state in Palestine for the

---

[38] Editors of Kingfisher. (2001). The Concise History Encyclopedia. Kingfisher.

displaced minority. During the 1930s, Jews from European states came to Palestine to settle in their promised homeland and to escape persecution. The Balfour Declaration became the first source of conflict between the Arabs and the Jews as the Palestinians refused to leave their homeland for the formation of a Jewish state.[39]

The 1948 Nakba—The Catastrophe: The Jewish population increased after World War II as ships full of Jewish settlers came to Palestine. The British government restricted the number of settlers allowed into Palestine, which led to the formation of extremist groups such as the Haganah and the Irgun, who bombed the Arabs and the British in retaliation. It was the setting stone for a chain of drastic events remembered as the 1948 Nakba (Catastrophe). In 1947, the U.N. passed the resolution for forming separate Jewish and Palestinian states, to which the Jews agreed, but the Arabs did not. As a result of the increasing conflicts and unable to handle the political situation, Britain gave up its mandate in 1948. Israeli leaders declared the creation of a Jewish state, and the United States and the Soviet Union immediately recognized Israel. However, that led to the Arab League states attacking Israel and starting a war that cost the Palestinians heavily. An estimated 700,000 Palestinians were driven out of their homes, which amounts to about 75% of their total population.[40]

---

[39] McGreal, C. (2023). What are the roots of the Israel-Palestine conflict? | Israel-Gaza war. The Guardian. https://www.theguardian.com/world/2023/nov/09/why-israel-palestine-conflict-history

[40] Israel Gaza war: History of the conflict explained. (2019). BBC News. https://www.bbc.com/news/newsbeat-44124396

The Six-Day War: In June 1967, the conflict between Israel and Egypt led to the Six-Day War. Israel inflicted air strikes on Egypt, and as a result, Jordan joined Egypt in fighting back. Israel had the upper hand in that war as it destroyed Egypt's air power and seized control of Gaza, Sinai, the Golan Heights, and the Palestinian East Jerusalem.[41]

The Yom Kippur War: In retaliation for the captured territories in the Six-Day War, the Arab states, led by Syria and Egypt, attacked Israel on the Yom Kippur holy day in October 1973. Initially, the Arabs were gaining ground but were soon overpowered by the Israeli militia, aided by the United States and its allies. Both sides suffered heavy losses. A peace treaty was signed later in 1978, meditated by then-U.S. President Jimmy Carter. Israel withdrew from the Sinai territory, and talks were carried out for Palestinian self-government in Gaza and the West Bank.[42]

First Intifada—Palestinian Uprising in 1987: A Palestinian uprising led by guerilla warriors resulted in severe crackdowns by the Israeli military. The region was subjected to a state of terror and uncertainty, resulting in deaths on both sides. The first of the two pacts was signed between Israel and the Palestine Liberation Organization (PLO) to avoid further conflict. These pacts were

---

[41] Westfall, S., Murphy, B., Taylor, A., Pietsch, B., & Salcedo, A. (2023). History of the Israeli-Palestine conflict: A chronology. The Washington Post. https://www.washingtonpost.com/world/2023/israel-palestine-conflict-timeline-history-explained/

[42] The October Arab-Israeli War of 1973: What happened? (2018). Al Jazeera. https://www.aljazeera.com/features/2018/10/8/the-october-arab-israeli-war-of-1973-what-happened

known as the Oslo Accords and based on the United Nations resolution for peace.

Second Intifada 2000: The peace didn't last long, and the Second Intifada began in 2000 when Ariel Sharon, an Israeli right-wing politician, stormed the Al Aqsa Mosque compound with a thousand heavily armed police and soldiers. Another reason for sparking the uprising was the reluctance of the Israeli government to abide by the Oslo Accords. Instead of following the pact to liberate Palestine, Israeli settlements increased in the West Bank and Gaza, which led the Palestinians to revolt. The conflicts and riots lasted till 2005.[43]

Hamas Election in 2006: In 2006, Hamas won the majority in the legislative elections in Gaza, a year after Israel withdrew its troops. It created political strains between Hamas and the Fatah Party, which had support in the West Bank. In 2007, Hamas seized control of Gaza, which resulted in a sixteen-year blockade by Israel on the small strip overcrowded with Palestinian refugees. This act began the humanitarian crisis and is referred to as apartheid by the Amnesty International Report.[44]

Conflicts 2008-2018: A series of conflicts prevented peace from being restored to Israel and Palestine. In 2008, Israel attacked Gaza, which lasted about three weeks. As a result, more than 1,110 Palestinians and at least 13 Israelis were killed. In

---

[43] Adam, A. (2020). Palestinian Intifada: How Israel orchestrated a bloody takeover | Conflict News. Al Jazeera. https://www.aljazeera.com/news/2020/9/28/palestinian-intifada-20-years-later-israeli-occupation-continues

[44] McGreal, C. (2023). What are the roots of the Israel-Palestine conflict? | Israel-Gaza war. The Guardian. https://www.theguardian.com/world/2023/nov/09/why-israel-palestine-conflict-history

2012, Hamas military chief Ahmed Jabari was assassinated by Israel, starting another severe torrent of air strikes between Israel and Gaza. At least 150 Palestinians and six Israelis were murdered.

In retaliation, Hamas killed three Israeli teenagers in 2014, which started another seven-week conflict, leaving 2,200 Palestinians dead in Gaza and 73 dead in Israel. Outrage and protests began in Gaza when the U.S. recognized Jerusalem as Israel's capital. Israeli troops kill more than 170 protesters over several months. In these ten years of conflict, the death toll of Palestinians was comparatively much higher than the Israelis.[45]

Israeli Raid on Al Aqsa Mosque in 2021: Israel raided the Al Aqsa Mosque in 2021, which led to Hamas firing thousands of rockets in retaliation. It started the deadliest conflict since 2014, in which more than 200 people were killed in Gaza, with only ten casualties on the other side. In January 2023, Israel raided the Palestinian city of Jenin and killed nine civilians in a shootout. Later, a Palestinian gunman killed seven people in the East Jerusalem Synagogue.

Hamas Attack on 7th October 2023: Fueled by the conflicts that had not stopped since the Jenin raid and the apartheid inflicted by the Israeli government, Hamas retaliated on 7th October 2023 by breaching the wall separating Gaza from Israeli settlements and launched a coordinated attack. About 1,400 Israeli deaths were reported as a result of Hamas' attack, and

---

[45] Westfall, S., Murphy, B., Taylor, A., Pietsch, B., & Salcedo, A. (2023). History of the Israeli-Palestine conflict: A chronology. The Washington Post. https://www.washingtonpost.com/world/2023/israel-palestine-conflict-timeline-history-explained/

Israeli Prime Minister Benjamin Netanyahu declared war on 8th October 2023.[46]

Ongoing Genocide of Palestinians: Since the open declaration of war, Israel has continued to bomb the densely populated areas of Gaza and the West Bank. The Palestinian death toll has risen to over thirty thousand people, including women and children. Despite the resolutions passed by the United Nations for a Ceasefire, Israel continues to bomb and eradicate the Palestinian population, committing the deadliest genocide of the 21st Century.

There are several reasons why there seems to be no achievable end to the conflicts between Israel and Palestine. The foremost reason is that both the Israeli and Palestinian nationalists want to take control of the same area, refusing to settle for a division of states.

Security issues led to the ethnic cleansing of Palestinians, which fueled the conflict and led to more revolts. The future is uncertain, but if the political situation continues on this dangerous track, there will be no two-state solution and no peace for Israel and Palestine.

The extreme policies inflicted by the Israeli government suggest that as long as Palestinians refuse to abandon their homeland, the tortuous killings, starvation, and genocide will continue. The lack of control exercised by the United Nations and the unhelpful involvement of Israel and Palestine's allies only

---

[46] Barghouti, M. (2023). On October 7, Gaza broke out of prison | Gaza . Al Jazeera. https://www.aljazeera.com/opinions/2023/10/14/on-october-7-gaza-broke-out-of-prison

worsen the situation. The world demands a ceasefire in Gaza and the West Bank. Even now, the genocide of Palestinians continues, indicating that we have failed as an advanced human civilization in this modern day and age.[47]

---

[47] Walt, S. M. (2024). Why the Israel-Palestine Conflict Won't End Any Time Soon. Foreign Policy. https://foreignpolicy.com/2024/01/08/israel-palestine-conflict-gaza-hamas/

Chapter 4: Stages of Genocide

"A genocide begins with the killing of one man — not for what he has done, but because of who he is."

- Kofi Annan

Genocide has existed since the advent of time and human existence on earth. But its prevailing existence and our failure as humanity to eliminate such heinous evil, even now in the progressive Twenty-first Century, raises several questions.

Firstly, what is the logic behind genocide, and what are the reasons that lead to it? Is it always a case of human killing instinct, or some other reasons, such as political power dynamics, that can also give birth to such deadly extermination of human lives? Is genocide a form of political violence, and if so, then why don't political leaders resort to other strategies to control the minorities without wiping them out? Why does a powerful majority feel threatened by a minority that is much lesser in number and inferior in power than them? Why do people stand by and allow genocides to happen, and what are the challenges faced by international intervention? Last but not least, how can we stop genocide as a collective and responsible human society?

When one studies the history of all genocidal conflicts that have occurred worldwide, questions like these and others come up, most of which have gone unanswered.

In this chapter, we will look at the reasons why genocides occur, the stages of genocide, as well as the typical patterns of genocide that the world has witnessed so far.

Reasons Why Genocide Occurs

The previous chapter discussed the role of human killing instinct in initiating genocide, but instincts are not always responsible for a stronger group to eliminate the weak. Personal survival might be a big reason for wars, but the cases of genocide are far more complex than two groups going to war with each other. The losses on either side are unequal, and so is the power balance, resulting in the ultimate destruction of the weaker group.

Some of the reasons behind genocides, such as the Rwandan genocide, Armenian genocide, the Holocaust, and Bosnian genocide, are discussed below:

Ideology and Extremism: The most common reason for genocides that have taken place in recent history are ideologies that promote extremism. One group dominates the others and asserts its power by committing crimes against them and causing them to surrender to the incessant violence inflicted on them. From Fascism and Nationalism that led to the Second World War and the Holocaust, Zionism that led to the brutal ethnic cleansing of Palestinians, Communism that led to the massacre of millions of Chinese, and Hindu Extremism that caused Hindu-Muslim conflicts in India, these ideologies promoted genocide and unleashed the worst crimes upon minority groups that were trampled in their wake.[48]

Political Strategies: Genocide has been used as a tool for conquest and a political strategy in controlling people belonging

[48] Editors of Kingfisher. (2001). The Concise History Encyclopedia. Kingfisher.

to a different race, color, or ethnicity as compared to the powerful majority group. A recent example is the Bharati Janta Party's support to Hindu extremists in cleansing the Muslim minority from India. Some strategies they have used so far include mob lynching in the name of religion and the Citizenship Amendment Act, which has recently been dubbed the Anti-Muslim Citizenship Act. To gain votes from the majority of the Hindu extremists, the BJP continues to use such tools to express their discrimination against Muslim minority groups.[49]

Scapegoating and Propaganda: Another reason that leads to genocide is scapegoating and propaganda, which is used to blame minorities for social insecurity, state instability, disease or pandemic, and other political and social issues. Thus, propaganda becomes the tool to turn the majority against a specific group, as seen in the Holocaust and the Armenian Genocide. The Armenians were labeled to be carriers of tuberculosis microbes, which made it seem rational to kill them in order to protect the majority of the population against the disease. Similarly, the Nazi Germans blamed the Jews for starting World War I and causing instability in Germany, which led to the Holocaust and extreme torture of the Jews in concentration camps.[50]

Ethnic and Cultural Cleansing: Ethnic cleansing and cultural conflicts can also result in genocide. A stronger ethnic group

---

[49] Sarwar, M. (2022). India's National Register of Citizens: A Tool for Muslim Disenfranchisement – Synergy: The Journal of Contemporary Asian Studies. Synergy: The Journal of Contemporary Asian Studies. https://utsynergyjournal.org/2022/01/17/indias-national-register-of-citizens-a-tool-for-muslim-disenfranchisement/

[50] Koonz, C., & Kissi, E. (2005). Auschwitz: Inside the Nazi State. Understanding Auschwitz Today. PBS: Public Broadcasting Service. https://www.pbs.org/auschwitz/understanding/origins.html

might eliminate the weaker group by eliminating their culture, language, and basis of existence. An example of this ethnic cleansing is the conflicts between Spain and Catalonia, which can be labeled as a cultural genocide. Catalonians were repressed and persecuted after the Spanish Civil War by the Francoist regime. Their culture, language, and architecture were destroyed by extremist Spaniards who considered them beneath them in status and power. In General Franco's regime in post-war Spain, the Catalonian language was banned, and severe fines were imposed on civilians who still used it. It was also banned in schools, libraries, museums, etc., and most of the cultural heritage of Catalonia was destroyed.[51]

Self-Preservation and Fear: Aside from the "Us vs. Them" mentality that plants the seed for genocidal conflicts, another reason is the "Destroy Them to Save Us" mentality. The fear of a particular group can cause people to polarize and attempt to wipe them out as a means of self-preservation. This fear can relate to both a fear of personal survival and a fear of pollution, which is further elaborated in "Purification." Examples from recent history include the Israel-Palestine conflict in which Israel claims to retaliate to preserve its state solidarity and civilian security from terrorist groups (Hamas) being supported by Palestinians.[52]

---

[51] Vilanova, F. (2017). Did Catalonia endure a (cultural) genocide? Journal of Catalan Intellectual History, 11, 15–32. https://doi.org/10.1515/jocih-2016-0002

[52] Straus, S. (2012). "Destroy Them to Save Us": Theories of Genocide and the Logics of Political Violence. Terrorism and Political Violence, 4, 544–560. https://doi.org/10.1080/09546553.2012.700611

Purification: Another theory behind the potential causes of genocide is Purification. This concept originated in the Enlightenment era, in which the extermination of a particular group of people was essential to achieving a perfect society. This purification to achieve a utopian state in which only one group exists and has power while the other groups are cleansed also led to genocide. The genocide of native Americans, the Catalonian massacres, the Holocaust, the Armenian Genocide, and the Rwandan genocide are all examples of purification.[53]

The instigators of this type of genocide strongly believe that they are doing the world a favor by eliminating a specific group of people. Hitler also had similar beliefs as he referred to Jews as a virus corrupting the world and stated in his book *Mein Kampf* that Jews were the "ferment of social decay," and it was his mission to eradicate them. Similarly, Vladimir Lenin of The Soviet Union dehumanized the Kulaks by referring to them as leeches sucking the blood of the working class. He also believed in purifying the state by getting rid of the Kulaks and the bureaucracy itself.[54]

Population Control: Controlling surplus populations by getting rid of a particular ethnic or racial group can also lead to genocide. The recent case of the Uyghur minority in China is an example of forced population control through sterilization

---

[53] Maritz, D. (2012). What Are the Main Causes of Genocide? E-International Relations. https://www.e-ir.info/2012/07/12/what-are-the-main-causes-of-genocide/

[54] Koenigsberg, R. (2015). Hitler, Lenin—and the Desire to Destroy "Parasites. Library of Social Science. https://www.libraryofsocialscience.com/newsletter/posts/2015/2015-03-06-hitler-lenin.html

programs, intrauterine devices (IUDs), and abortions as part of a systematic effort to reduce the Uyghur birth rate.[55]

COVID-19 is also considered by many as an example of biological warfare by spreading the pandemic and delaying the invention of vaccines to limit the overall global population.

Stages of Genocide

Genocide does not occur immediately. Instead, it takes place in multiple stages, from the early warning signs to the deadly execution of crimes against humanity. In every genocide that has taken place in the world so far, these stages were constant, be it the Darfur genocide and Palestinian genocide of the Twenty-first Century or the unacknowledged Armenian genocide and the massacre of indigenous Americans.[56]

The different stages of genocide, as explained by George H. Stanton, are discussed below:

1. **Classification:** The first stage is the classification of a particular ethnicity, race, religion, or nationality as the other group. As a result, the "Us vs. Them" mentality rises and identifies the groups on the basis of their culture, language, religion, etc. Genocide is more likely to occur in bipolar societies that lack a cohesive, unified identity. For example, Hitler

---

[55] Wang, M. (2023). China's 'beautiful Xinjiang' continues to oppress Uighurs | Opinions. Al Jazeera. https://www.aljazeera.com/opinions/2023/9/12/chinas-beautiful-xinjiang-continues-to-oppress-uighurs

[56] Stanton, G. H. (2016). 10 Stages of Genocide. Genocide Watch. http://genocidewatch.net/genocide-2/8-stages-of-genocide/

classified the Jews as the other group, setting the earliest foundation for the Jewish Holocaust.

2. **Symbolization:** The second stage is symbolization, which refers to both the stereotyping of the classified group and the symbolic representation of why they deserve to be excluded from society. Jews in Nazi Germany were forced to wear yellow stars to symbolize their identity as Jews, which made them a target of hatred, social exclusion, and public humiliation.[57]

3. **Discrimination:** As tensions between the two groups increase, the third stage, known as Discrimination, occurs. The majority group discriminates strongly against the minority and asserts their dominance through all means possible. Their facilities and rights are restricted, they are openly scorned, and their status in society is reduced to zero. The apartheid in the United States is a clear example of discrimination against African Americans and people of color by the white supremacist majority. Discrimination against the Tutsi ethnic group in Rwanda was also an early contributor to the Rwandan genocide.

4. **Dehumanization:** The fourth stage of genocide is the dehumanization of the target group to normalize their elimination. By reducing their status as human beings and comparing them to vermin, pests, parasites, and other such elements, the influential group rationalizes genocide on a psychological level. Thus, dehumanization overcomes the human revulsion to murdering their own species. Moral exclusion is also

---

[57] The ten stages of genocide. (n.d.). Holocaust Memorial Day Trust. Retrieved March 19, 2024, from https://www.hmd.org.uk/learn-about-the-holocaust-and-genocides/what-is-genocide/the-ten-stages-of-genocide/

a form of dehumanization in which the victim group is considered outside the boundary where ethical and social values apply.[58]

Dehumanization has been both a stage and a common element of genocide in human history. Hitler compared the Jews to 'vermin and parasites,' the Tutsi were compared to 'cockroaches,' the enslaved Africans were referred to as 'monkeys,' and the indigenous Americans were labeled as 'not fully evolved to be called humans.' These examples strengthen the beliefs of the powerful majority group that eliminating the target group would cleanse their society.[59]

5. **Organization:** Organization is the fifth stage of genocide after dehumanization and the psychological acceptance of killing the target group. Such acts of mass killing are always organized (usually by the state) and planned. Hitler's rearmament of Germany in the late 1930s is an example of organization before genocide. The Sudanese government supported and armed the Janjaweed, who became the major contributors to the Darfur genocide.

6. **Polarization:** Polarization, the sixth stage, refers to spreading more hate between the two groups through propaganda, hate speech, slurs, etc. At this stage, the two groups strongly oppose each other and stand on the brink of bloodied conflict. To polarize the nationalist German majority, the Nazis

---

[58] Newman, L. S. (2019). Confronting Humanity at Its Worst (pp. 119–123). Oxford University Press, USA.

[59] Weindling, P. J. (2000). Eradicating Parasites. In Epidemics and Genocide in Eastern Europe, 1890–1945 (pp. 19–48). Oxford University Press. http://dx.doi.org/10.1093/acprof:oso/9780198206910.003.0016

used the Der Stürmer newspaper to propagate the hatred for the Jewish minority further.

7. Preparation: No genocide can occur without preparation. Weapons are stocked up, strategies are made, and execution plans are derived to eliminate the target group once and for all. This is the seventh stage of genocide, and an example from history denoting it is the Final Solution by Hitler, in which he prepared for the upcoming Holocaust by setting up concentration camps such as Auschwitz, Buchenwald, and Dachau.

8. Persecution: From the eighth stage, called Persecution, the crimes against the target group begin. Victims suffer from biological and economic genocide. Properties are confiscated, and people are segregated and starved. Thus, the horrors of genocide are unleashed freely in this stage, and the target group is repressed by all means.

9. Extermination: The most brutal stage of them all is extermination, in which the complete eradication of the particular ethnic, racial, or religious group becomes the sole motive of the perpetrators. The extermination of European Jews in Nazi concentration camps wiped out a significant part of the Jewish population. They were tortured till their last breath, and those who survived were forced to work as slaves. Even today, in the ongoing genocide of the Uyghur Muslims and the Palestinians, the powerful groups are using all means possible to wipe out the population of the victim groups totally.

10. Denial: The last stage of genocide is denial. The perpetrators and their later generations refuse to take responsibility for the atrocious crimes they committed against the target groups. Evidences are covered, and witnesses are intimidated to wipe out any remembrance of the heinous acts that took place against the specific weaker group. Examples include the Armenian genocide and how it is being fervently denied to this day, the genocide in Cambodia under the Khmer Rouge regime, and the famine-genocide of Holodomor in Soviet Ukraine. The scale of the mass killing is often denied or undermined by the perpetrators, and they try to justify their acts even years after the genocide.[60]

These stages are the ten warning signs of genocide and should be nipped in the bud before things take a toll and the situation worsens for both groups.

The Ten Patterns of Genocide

Aside from the stages of genocide are the ten patterns of genocide, which refer to the common crimes that take place during genocides. Like a pattern, the repetition of these crimes is witnessed in genocides of the past and present. Genocide is both a systematic and patterned infliction of mass violence, and the ten patterns are discussed below:

1. **Gendered Atrocity:** Both men and women are massacred, which is also known as gender-neutral mass murder. However, both genders might be treated differently before murder. Such

---

[60] Matulewska, A., & Gwiazdowicz, D. J. (2021). In Quest of Genocide Understanding: Multiple Faces of Genocide | International Journal for the Semiotics of Law - Revue internationale de Sémiotique juridique. SpringerLink. https://link.springer.com/article/10.1007/s11196-021-09847-5

as, men could be tortured before killing them, and women would have to suffer sexual violence as well.

2. **Mass Murder of Battle-aged Men + Atrocities against Women and Children:** The patriarchal social structure is decapitated by killing all men and boys, leaving only women and female children to watch the horrors and suffer violence at the hands of their perpetrators.

3. **Gendercide:** Also known as sex-selective violence, either men or women are killed while the other gender is left alive in barely livable conditions.

4. **Sexualized Violence:** Mass rape and sexual violence against all genders and age groups falls in this category. The assailants inflict sexual torture on their victims until death or severe physical and mental damage.

5. **Mass Cultural Destruction + Human Rights Violations:** Another pattern is the complete destruction of culture and the violation of human rights. Important institutions, symbols, and political or other figures of the target group are destroyed publicly to spread more fear in the hearts of the survivors.

6. **Genocide by Attrition:** Man-made famine, artificial weather conditions, and blockade of medical resources to weaken and torture the target group are referred to as genocide by attrition. It is a slow but painful destruction of the target group in which the perpetrators eat away at their existence through artificial disasters.

7. **Ecocide:** Destroying the ecology and environment of the areas where the target groups reside is known as ecocide. The atomic bomb attacks on Hiroshima and Nagasaki not only

resulted in mass killings but also damaged the environment irreparably for decades to come. Nuclear radiation left the land infertile and dangerous for human survival.

8. **Appropriation + Destruction of Biological Resources:** Biological resources like water, agriculture, fossil fuel, etc., are denied to the group suffering from genocide. A relevant example is how Israel regulates the biological resources of food and water that are permissible to Gaza and other Palestinian territories.

9. **Denial + Prevention of Identity:** Denial can mean the refusal to commit genocide as well as denying the fundamental human identity to a specific minority group. They are reduced to living as refugees and are deprived of human rights and identity.

10. **Killing through Work:** Killing the remaining members of the group through slavery and hard manual labor is also a pattern of genocide. This has occurred in both the Holocaust and the apartheid in the US.

These patterns overlap each other and can occur at the same time or separately throughout the different stages of genocide. However, the violence and trauma that is unleashed on the target groups during these patterns exhibit why genocide is known as the worst of all crimes against humanity. The psychological effects of genocide transcend generations and leave a dark and morbid stain on the history of humankind.[61]

---

[61] Joeden-Forge, E. von. (2023). 10 Patterns of Genocide. Lemkin Institute. https://www.lemkininstitute.com/ten-patterns-of-genocide

Chapter 5: Genocide in Western Society

"Why is it that, as a culture, we are more comfortable seeing two men holding guns than holding hands?"

- Ernest Gaine

Western society is often regarded as a symbol of progress, prosperity, and development. The ethos of humanitarianism, magnanimity, and world peace originate from the West and are widely propagated to be the way forward for humans in this advanced 21st century. The Western ideals regarding a progressive world focus on all humans being perceived as equal regardless of their race, ethnicity, or religion. This equality guarantees them the same fundamental rights: freedom and the ability to live a life of dignity and respect.

However, historical accounts prove that despite focusing on these values in theory, Western culture has failed to implement them practically. In most of the genocides that have occurred throughout the world, the West has been a major contributor — not as a champion of peace but as a supporter of the perpetrators and a silent witness to genocide. Even if they have managed to limit and eradicate the possibility of a genocide occurring in the West, their controversial involvement on the political eve of several known cases of genocide in third-world countries has sparked debate.

The ongoing genocide of Palestine is a clear example of Western involvement and the ironic clash with their apparent values of peace and acceptance. Israel is not the only state receiving military assistance and weapons from the US to commit genocide. The cases of Cambodia and East Timor stand as a testament to Western involvement in the execution of genocides. Even if we leave the cases taking place in the 20th century and look back at the past, the root cause of genocide and mass killings also originated from the West in the form of conquests, wars for imperial dominance, and later colonialism.[62]

State of Genocide in Western Society

There have been no recent cases of genocide in Western democracies. However, genocide in and of itself is a strong term. Its definition as the deliberate persecution of people belonging to a particular race, ethnicity, or religion excludes it from being applied to all cases of mass killings.

Easy access to weapons and firearms in the US has led to school shootouts and other acts of terrorism, but they can not be referred to as genocide. As explained earlier in Chapter 2, terrorism and hate crimes are separate from genocide due to a difference in the reasons causing the crime. Genocide is the total eradication of a particular group, while terrorism is spreading terror through violence. We can find several recent accounts of terrorism in Western democracies, but none of genocide.

According to Rudolph Rummel, a researcher from the Department of Political Science at the University of Hawaii, genocides occur through the abuse of immense power. He states that *'power kills and absolute power kills absolutely.'* Therefore,

---

[62] Rumney, P. N. S. (1997). Getting Away with Murder: Genocide and Western State Power. The Modern Law Review, Vol. 60, No. 4 (Jul. 1997), Pp. 594-608. https://doi.org/http://www.jstor.org/stable/1097218

the reason he suggests behind no recent cases of genocide in Western countries is the fostering of a strong democracy. In a strong democratic state, the power balance is distributed among the people, and the restriction of checks of power among the political elite reduces the risk of genocide. In such a system, the judiciary is independent of the executive powers. Thus, even if a specific group is targeted, the case is brought to court and dealt with accordingly. He concludes his research on power, genocide, and mass murder by proposing that democratic freedom and awareness about the repercussions of genocide and other hate crimes can be the only solutions to putting an end to genocide.[63]

After the Holocaust in World War II, the West seemingly awakened to a dire need to establish peace. Thus, peace was achieved in Western society by propagating the ideals of humanitarianism, fair legal systems, and world peace. However, it does not exempt the political powers of the Western World from partaking in genocide in developing countries by supporting military regimes, changing the narrative through global media, and standing as a silent witness to the crimes being committed.

During the Cambodian genocide, the British government allegedly supported the military regime inflicted by the Khmer Rouge. The SAS provided military training to members of the Cambodian Non-Communist Resistance, who later went on to commit genocide against the native Cambodians. Similarly, it is debated among scholars studying genocide that the US is complicit in the Indonesian occupation of East Timor as it

---

[63] Rummel, R. J. (1994). Power, Genocide and Mass Murder. Journal of Peace Research, Vol. 31, No. 1 (Feb., 1994), Pp. 1-10.
https://doi.org/https://www.jstor.org/stable/425578

provided military support to the perpetrators and prevented the United Nations from taking action against the Indonesians oppressing the natives of East Timor.[64]

Other relevant examples of genocides ignored or supported by the West are the Armenian genocide, the Darfur genocide, and, most recently, the Palestinian genocide.

Colonialism

A by-product of the European explorers, mainly the Spanish, British, French, Dutch, and Portuguese empires, colonialism became a cause of mass killings in the East and other underdeveloped countries as these settlers gained more control in the region through political dominance. Starting from just a trading company or an expedition, colonizers took over land, resources, national treasures, and the freedom of the natives. The East India Company's transition to the British Raj in India is an undeniable example of the West seizing power in the East.

Colonialism resulted in British control over major regions of South Asia, Africa, and Australia. By just taking the example of colonialism in the Indian subcontinent, we can see how it marked some of the stages of genocide. The natives were labeled illiterate and inferior, creating a stark difference between them and the European settlers. This difference was further emphasized when white towns were created, differentiating the living conditions of the settlers and the natives. The Indian

[64] Rumney, P. N. S. (1997). Getting Away with Murder: Genocide and Western State Power. The Modern Law Review, Vol. 60, No. 4 (Jul. 1997), Pp. 594-608. https://doi.org/http://www.jstor.org/stable/1097218

population was used as a source of cheap labor and soldiers to serve in world wars, and the British infused their culture into the subcontinent heavily.[65]

In literal terms, colonialism might not be similar to genocide or mass killing. Still, it resulted in the mass killing of the natives. According to research by Sullivan and Hickel, the number of people killed in the forty years of British rule due to imperial policies surged to a massive 100 million Indians. Extreme poverty increased from twenty-three percent to more than fifty percent, and the life expectancy in India dropped from 26.7 years to 21.9 years. These figures suggest that an excessive number of people died during British rule, becoming the most significant number of policy-induced deaths in human history.[66]

American Civil War

The American Civil War began in 1861 and lasted about four years. The primary cause behind this war was the rising tensions between northern and southern states on the issues of slavery, state autonomy, and further westward expansion. The drastic economic difference between the northern and southern states also became a significant factor in the people's revolt and the start of a war.[67]

---

[65] Editors of Kingfisher. (2001). The Concise History Encyclopedia. Kingfisher.

[66] Sullivan, D., & Hickel, J. (2022). How British colonialism killed 100 million Indians in 40 years | History | Al Jazeera. https://www.aljazeera.com/opinions/2022/12/2/how-british-colonial-policy-killed-100-million-indians

[67] Editors of HISTORY. (2009). Civil War - Causes, Dates & Battles. HISTORY. https://www.history.com/topics/american-civil-war/american-civil-war-history

The Union forces (northern states) held a clear advantage over the Confederates and eventually gained victory in 1865. The Civil War was dubbed the deadliest war in American history, as over 620,000 people were killed, with a large number of unmentioned civilian deaths. The actual figure was much higher and is claimed to be around 650,000 to 850,000 casualties, as suggested in recent quantitative research by Dr. David Hacker at the University of Minnesota. The southern death toll was also much higher than the 258,000 deaths officially recorded.[68]

While this war can not be stated as a genocide, it was a conflict between two groups, each with the intent to wipe out the other. The loss of lives and economic downfall that resulted from this war pushed America decades back.

The Aboriginal Australians

Another case of potential genocide that is not mentioned enough in history is the wipeout of Aboriginal Australians. During the first 140 years of British settlement on the continent, at least 270 massacres of Aboriginal Australians have been documented by researchers. These massacres and the cruelty suffered by the Aborigines can all be categorized as genocide. Children were forcibly removed from their homes, and their cultural identity was wiped out. This oppression has been referred to as the Stolen Generations of Australia. Their language was banned, and people

---

[68] Zeller, B. (2022). How Many Died in the American Civil War? HISTORY. https://www.history.com/news/american-civil-war-deaths

were jailed for communicating in it, leading to the extinction of the tribal Aboriginal language in the 20th century.[69]

Former Australian Prime Minister Kevin Rudd offered a public apology in 2008, but it could not reverse the years of damage and destruction suffered by the Aborigines. This is another case of genocide and mass murder inflicted by the West that was forgotten over time.

Biological and Chemical Warfare

Causing the spread of diseases, pandemics, and famine are methods of biological warfare. These tactics have been used from ancient history, as accounts exist of the Carthaginian general Hannibal using snakes and scorpions as weapons, Roman Emperor Frederick Barbarossa contaminating water supplies to get rid of the opponents, and the Mongols throwing dead bodies infected by the plague in enemy boundaries.[70]

These methods of biological warfare date as far back as 600 BC, while the most recent case is debatably the COVID-19 outbreak. Even in the World Wars, plague, biological herbicides, and other diseases were used to kill people and weaken the enemy. Several countries developed biological weapons programs during World War II to experiment with biological warfare, which was later allegedly implemented in the Korean

---

[69] Blakemore, E. (2023). Who are Aboriginal Australians—and why are they still fighting for recognition? Culture. https://www.nationalgeographic.com/culture/article/aboriginal-australians

[70] Dowdeswell, M. (2023). 6 Crazy Examples of Biological Warfare Used throughout History. TheCollector. https://www.thecollector.com/crazy-examples-of-biological-warfare-throughout-history/

War and the Gulf War. These methods were used for their invisibility and delayed effects, causing fear and panic among whole populations. It became much simpler for people to be killed by a pandemic rather than dropping a bomb to wipe them out and then shouldering the blame for it.[71]

Chemical warfare includes using toxins, gas, blistering agents, and other chemical weapons to wipe out opponents. It was widely used in World War I, as the recent invention of helicopters was used to spray large areas of people with poisonous fumes, causing diseases and death. Gas masks became a necessity of the war, and the world saw destruction through chemical means for the first time. Phosgene, sulfur mustard, and lewisites caused 1.2 million casualties in World War I. Later, these methods of chemical warfare were also used in the Vietnam War by the US and in the 1980s during the Iran-Iraq War, where a single chemical warfare attack on the Kurdish civilian population of Halabja resulted in 5000 deaths. Similar to genocide, it was a targeted attack on people belonging to a particular ethnicity.[72]

Impact of Genocide on Western Society

Genocide creates a lasting impact on the people affected by it, as well as the global population witnessing its horror. The Holocaust is a relevant example of the guilt of committing genocide, impacting the nation and its future generations.

---

[71] Riedel, S. (2004). Biological Warfare and Bioterrorism: A Historical Review. *Baylor University Medical Center Proceedings, 4,* 400–406. https://doi.org/10.1080/08998280.2004.11928002

[72] Ganesan, K., Raza, S. K., & Vijayaraghavan, R. (2010). Chemical warfare agents. Journal of Pharmacy And Bioallied Sciences, 3, 166. https://doi.org/10.4103/0975-7406.68498

Postwar Germany has strived to build a new national identity based on democracy, human rights, and international cooperation. Aside from providing a public apology to the Jews and the world, the Germans also modified their national anthem to eradicate Nazi ideals (a superior German state) from their identity and preserved history in the form of architecture and monuments to warn the world about the consequences of genocide. The slogan *'Never Again'* symbolizes their efforts against antisemitism, racism, and hatred.[73]

Similarly, the survivors of genocide also suffer from its lasting impacts, such as the European Jewish community, the Darfurs, Bosniaks, Rohingyas, etc. Most of them were reduced to the status of refugees in the aftermath of genocides, and it took them years to overcome the trauma and start living as free citizens.

Genocide disrupts global peace, increases humanitarian crises, and results in the loss of life and valuable cultural heritage. Thus, we must unite against the worst of all evils and ensure that it doesn't occur again. The Western society preaches ideals of peace, human rights, and tolerance. However, these ideals hold little weight without concrete action. Practical implementation, not only within their boundaries but throughout the world, is necessary to stop genocide. By working together, we can strive towards a future where *'Never Again'* becomes more than just a slogan but a reality.

[73] Port, A. I. (2023). Never Again. Harvard University Press.

Chapter 6: Genocide in Eastern Society

"A combination of revolution and war is the cauldron for genocide."

- Robert Melson

Eastern society contradicts the West in multiple aspects. Both cultures differ in their political systems, religious influences, and ideological concepts. While the West has adapted to a tolerant ideology of *'Equality for All'* and Democracy, most of the East still relies on Purification and Militarism.

Although war cannot be deemed as genocide, an unavoidable connection exists between the two. Genocide is a tool used to propagate fear during wars, as organized mass murder is carried out to reduce the numbers of the opposing side. Most major cases of genocide in the East, such as the Herero genocide, the Armenian genocide, Rwandan and Bosnian genocide, all take place during wars.[74]

This chapter focuses on the cases of genocide occurring in the Eastern world, the root causes of genocide, the different political systems, the overall comparison of the East's situation to the West, and the impact of genocide on Eastern society.

---

[74] Straus, S. (2012). "Destroy Them to Save Us": Theories of Genocide and the Logics of Political Violence. Terrorism and Political Violence, 4, 544–560. https://doi.org/10.1080/09546553.2012.700611

State of Genocide in Eastern Society

Genocide has been deeply rooted in the Eastern world. From the bloodthirsty Assyrians to the modern Communist regimes, mass killing and eradication of particular races, cultures, ethnicities, or religions has been very common. Most cases of genocide in the East were never fully resolved, such as the Israel-Palestine conflict that resulted in more than thirty thousand deaths in 2024.

The origins of genocide in the East can be traced back to ancient invaders who sought land and power in the vast and fertile eastern region. Warrior nations like the Assyrians, the Aryans, and the Mongols seized land and killed the natives brutally. The concept of human sacrifices was also observed in most of the ancient tribes living in these lands, resulting in the death of thousands of innocent people.[75]

The diverse political systems existing in the East also made it more susceptible to genocide. From Imperialism, Colonialism, Militarism, and Communism, the East has suffered the consequences of each, mainly resulting in human deaths and destruction.

Imperialism

Imperialism is defined as a form of international hierarchy in which one political community effectively governs or controls another political community. All the political power is held by a

[75] Editors of Kingfisher. (2001). The Concise History Encyclopedia. Kingfisher.

central figure, mainly the King, who presides as a supreme sovereign over all states falling under his Empire.[76]

From as far back as 4000 BCE, Imperialism has existed in the East. The Pharaohs in the Middle East, the Emperors of the Tang and Shang dynasties in China, the Assyrians, and the Babylonians all established imperial regimes. As a result, the people who stood against the government or threatened its dominion were eradicated through military force under the king's orders. The Assyrians were experts in warfare. Their conquests led to significant loss of life, destruction, and displacement of populations in the conquered regions. However, the precise figure of people killed and displaced in their regime is unknown.[77]

Aftermath of Colonialism

"Colonialism is not a thinking machine, nor a body endowed with reasoning faculties. It is violence in its natural state, and it will only yield when confronted with greater violence."

- Frantz Fanon

The majority of the mass killings caused in the East post-Middle Ages were due to Colonialism and European settlement in the region. The British Raj in India and the European colonies in Africa both caused genocide of the natives, exploiting them and their resources for their gains. Cultural genocide is also common in colonialism as the colonizing state imposes its own

---

[76] Lake, D. A. (2015). Imperialism. In International Encyclopedia of the Social & Behavioral Sciences (pp. 682–684). Elsevier. http://dx.doi.org/10.1016/B978-0-08-097086-8.93053-8

[77] Editors of Kingfisher. (2001). The Concise History Encyclopedia. Kingfisher.

culture and language on the colonies, reducing the significance of their traditions and native language.

The formation of nation-states in the Indian Subcontinent based on the Two Nation Theory led to one of the deadliest wars of independence ever seen, with millions of South Asians killed as a result. South Asia suffered from the bloodiest genocides of the region during the War of Independence in 1857, the India-Pakistan Independence in 1947, and the Bangladeshi Genocide in 1971. The root cause for these three massacres can be traced back to the Decolonization of the subcontinent and the unfair distribution of power and resources. The West had been involved in the roots of these genocides, but the factors of hatred based on ethnicity and religion set fuel to the fire.[78]

Colonialism vs. Imperialism

Most contemporary scholars argue that there is not much difference between colonialism and imperialism. Both systems are formed when a politically persuasive state takes control of other regions through conquests or economic endeavors, establishing its rule over its colonies or empire states. However, according to Barbara Arneil, a researcher from the Political Science Department at the University of British Columbia, colonialism can be distinguished from imperialism based on its ideology.

Imperialism focused solely on seizing lands and forming an empire governing a group of states entirely subjected to the King

---

[78] Jacob, F. (2019). Genocide and Mass Violence in Asia. Walter de Gruyter GmbH & Co KG.

or the highest political figure of the empire. On the other hand, colonialism was idealized as the need to improve the living conditions of backward people (natives) of the colonial states by infusing their own culture, language, and dominion over them.[79]

The Indian subcontinent has witnessed both Imperial and Colonial regimes. Under the Mughals, the last Imperial system of the subcontinent, there was no focus on improving living conditions or cultural and technological awareness of the general *awaam*. The rulers focused on expanding their empire and showcasing their grandeur through imperial architecture, but they should have taken more part in public service works. On the other hand, British colonialism in the region led to improved infrastructure, especially by introducing the railway system, establishing educational and vocational institutions to produce skilled workers, and a comparatively higher involvement in public service works than their imperial predecessors.[80]

Militarism

Militarism is defined as the belief that a country should have a strong military capability and be prepared to use it. In a military state, all the political power is vested in the military as it can make important decisions, impose new laws, invade other states, and establish its unquestioned dominance over the state and its

---

[79] Arneil, B. (2023). Colonialism versus Imperialism. Political Theory, 1, 146–176. https://doi.org/10.1177/00905917231193107

[80] Editors of Kingfisher. (2001). The Concise History Encyclopedia. Kingfisher.

civilians. In this system, the civilian authority is subordinated to the armed forces' decision.[81]

Military regimes have also played a crucial part in endangering the lives of civilians and causing genocidal acts in the Eastern world. Due to war and instability, military regimes were imposed on most eastern states, such as Pakistan, Iraq, and the Middle East. Some of the famous military dictators in the East are General Zia-ul-Haq of Pakistan, who brought his ideology of Islamism and forcefully imposed his regime; General Saddam Hussein of Iraq, who was accused of harboring weapons of mass destruction; and the former Egyptian president Hosni Mubarak who was ousted in 2011

Communism

"Communism, though this is not widely recognized either in the East or in the West, is the most modern and most virulent form of Western Imperialism."

- Bertrand Russell

Communism, born from nationalist ideologies, was a modern political system emphasizing all powers vested in the state. It is a political and economic system in which private property and a profit-based economy (two main features of Capitalism) are replaced with public ownership and communal control of all resources. Its main objective was to create a classless society that focused more on the progress and development of the state and

---

[81] Melby, C. K. (2020). Militarism . 1914-1918-Online. International Encyclopedia of the First World War (WW1). https://encyclopedia.1914-1918-online.net/article/militarism

the fulfillment of the basic human needs of every individual. However, this system failed due to the mechanization of human life, which caused people to revolt against it.[82]

An example of destruction caused by Communist regimes has already been discussed in Chapter 2. During the formation of the People's Republic of China under the philosophy of the Great Leap Forward by Mao Zedong, about 35 to 45 million Chinese were killed. Civilians opposing the communist regime were subjected to mass starvation, executions, and famine.

Comparisons to the West

Genocides in the East resulted from tyranny and a lack of strong democracy. However, most of these genocides gained traction due to Western involvement. Cases like the Cambodian genocide, the Darfurs, and the ongoing genocide of the Palestinians worsened as the international community failed to stop them, and the superpowers in the West stood alongside the perpetrators. Furthermore, the ideological elements of race, religion, expansion, and cultivation are deeply rooted in the East, which has resulted in more genocides being committed in this region as compared to the West.[83]

---

[82] Communism. (n.d.). Encyclopædia Britannica. Retrieved April 5, 2024, from https://www.britannica.com/topic/communism

[83] Kiernan, B. (2003). Twentieth-Century Genocides. In R. Gellately & B. Kiernan, The Specter of Genocide (pp. 29–52). Cambridge University Press. http://dx.doi.org/10.1017/cbo9780511819674.002

Impact of Genocide on Eastern Society

The main reason the East has failed to acquire the power and development seen in the West is the ongoing conflict and instability of the region. The frequency of genocides occurring in this region was much higher than that of the West and continues to this day.

The Eastern Society has not yet recovered from the horrors of genocide. It is unable to progress due to the consistent threat of life to its ethnic and religious minorities. The political ideologies of the region and the ongoing conflicts make it impossible to achieve a state of peace in the countries affected by genocide. Those who kill have the sole motive of leaving no witnesses behind. Those who survive become refugees and struggle even for their fundamental human rights. These refugees then have to flee to states that can grant them political asylum. Still, even then, they experience issues such as estrangement, discrimination, and a constant fear of being targeted again.

As most of the capital in eastern states is being spent on military reinforcement and defense purposes, the region's overall economy suffers. While there are countries like India and China that have struggled and eventually recovered from the impact of genocide, the majority of the Eastern world comprises developing and underdeveloped countries where mass killing and cultural oppression continue. Sinking under the burden of loans and financial aid from the World Bank and the IMF, the East still has a long way to go in reaching the same pedestal of progress and development compared to the West.

Chapter 7: Misuse of Religion

"Religion is regarded by the common people as true, by the wise as false, and by the rulers as useful."

- Lucius Annaeus Seneca

Religion is one of the few factors that unites people of different races, social classes, and ethnicities under a strong canopy, and it becomes an ideology that pushes them forward into action in the name of God.

Almost every religion condemns violence and hatred, yet it seems ironic that religion has often become the cause of wars and genocide. In the hands of a politician or a leading figure, it doesn't take long for the message of peace, love, and humanity to turn into a calling for violence and wiping out *others* (the non-believers or followers of other religions).

Most of the genocides that have occurred, such as the Bosnian and Rwandan genocide as well as the Holocaust, had religious influences in their foundations.

History is full of several accounts where religion became an agitating force for genocide and massacres, motivating the people to do God's work and prove themselves worthy of paradise, eternal liberation, or any such reward that is deemed most superior in their religion.

From the Crusades to the Inquisition, Islamic radicalism, and Hindu extremism, religion has been misused as a powerful political tool to fuel the masses into wiping out a particular group.

Fundamental Concept of Religion

The fundamental concept of religion, summed up in a few lines, is to have something or someone to believe in, a clear set of rules to follow, a designated religious place to worship, and to honor their faith and consider it supreme over all other aspects of life.

The word religion itself is defined as *"human beings' relation to that which they regard as holy, sacred, absolute, spiritual, divine, or worthy of special reverence. It is also commonly regarded as consisting of the way people deal with ultimate concerns about their lives and their fate after death."*[84]

There are two main classifications for the origin of religions: naturalistic and humanistic. In the early evolving civilizations, nature was considered the source of life, and people began to worship everything that sustained them.

For them, the sun was a god, and the rivers were god, as were the rains and the wind. In short, every natural phenomenon that kept them safe and alive became revered as a divine entity. These are the naturalistic origins of religion. An example of naturalistic religions can be Zoroastrians worshipping fire as it represents their god Ahura Mazda's divine light and energy, and the Aztecs worshipping the sun god and offering human sacrifices and other rituals to keep the balance of nature. Ancient Egyptian mythology also represents different elements of nature (sun, water, wind, earth, etc.) as gods.

---

[84] Religion. (n.d.). Encyclopædia Britannica. Retrieved from https://www.britannica.com/topic/religion

However, as humans became more civilized and began to use natural resources for their own benefits (through agriculture, travel, shelter, etc.), they embraced the concept that divine entities controlled natural things and humans were also part of nature, subjected to serve the gods above them.

These religions can be monotheistic and deem one God supreme over the entire cosmos (like Islam, Christianity, Judaism, etc.), or they could be polytheistic and preach about multiple gods, each carrying a duty to keep the balance of nature (like Hinduism, Taoism, Shenism, Shinto, etc.).

The primary function of religions is to organize people and teach them about life, the creation of the world, and the rewards for living virtuously, compared to the punishments for committing sin. It aims to answer humans' questions about their existence and purpose, aligning them with a greater reason for their presence and motivating them to serve the god they preach about.

However, it creates a sense of "Us vs. Them" between the people as they start viewing people with differing beliefs as their enemies, and in some cases, this hatred is used to turn them on the path of violence by politicians and religious leaders.

Politics and Religion

"Religion often is misused for purely power-political goals, including war."

- Hans Kung

Religion holds immense power over its followers and, as a result, can be used to manipulate them. Religious symbols and rhetoric have often been used by leaders to motivate their people to lay down their lives for a divine cause, such as religious war, expansion, or purification.

Religion and the state have often been interconnected when commanding the masses. We see this connection in Christianity and the Holy Roman Empire, where the monarchy and the missionaries worked together to rule over an ever-expanding group of people. Often, religion held an even greater power than the monarchy due to the superiority of God instilled into the hearts of the followers.

The Holocaust in World War II is not a religious genocide. Still, we cannot ignore the influence of religion in propagating it. In the decades preceding the Holocaust, Christian clergy often stressed the same anti-Judaism themes as the Nazis. They presented the Jews as materialistic people caring only about wealth and involved in the corruption of society, often referring to them as *parasitic* capitalists.

The seed planted by these teachings enabled the Nazis to exploit them for their own purposes and gain Christian support in eliminating the Jews and justifying their actions. They also presented the image of the Jew as the Christ-killer and their values as being opposite to Christianity.

Thus, the dehumanization of Jews had started decades before the Holocaust, and religious influences played an unavoidable role in it. Adolf Hitler also used Christian terminology in his speeches, claiming that he was chosen by Providence for the task of cleansing the world of all Jews.[85]

In 1921, Hitler addressed a National Socialist rally by stating: *"Those who want to keep our Christianity, which, alas, today is merely a Christianity of appearances rather than one of deeds, have to confront those who rob us of our Christianity."* His words show support for the Christians but, at the same time, bring the Jews into the picture as the enemy by calling them the robbers of Christianity.[86]

Although his message contrasted strikingly with the message of love and peace taught in Christianity, he was able to gain the favor of the masses by manipulating them through their faith. It led to him gaining political power as well by getting appointed as Chancellor in 1933, boosting the Nazis to become one of the strongest political parties in Germany. This political power and authority later led to the Nazis committing genocide without the fear of being held accountable.

Another example of misusing religion's power over the people for political gains is the conflict between Hindus and Muslims, which transcends to the conflict between India and Pakistan. General Zia-ul-Haq used the concept of Islamism to gain power and present himself as a chosen one to bring back the Islamic order in Pakistan. The majority of the Muslim population in Pakistan surrendered to his policies and autocratic reign without

---

[85] Bartov, O., & Mack, P. (2001). In God's Name: Genocide and Religion in the Twentieth Century. Berghahn Books.

[86] Munson, H. (2018). Christianity, Antisemitism, and the Holocaust. Religions, 1, 26. https://doi.org/10.3390/rel9010026

question, as they felt going against it would be seen as going against their religion.

A slightly different approach to using religion to gain political power can be seen in India. As India is a secular state by constitution, Zia's modus operandi of using religious influences to gain power could not be implemented.

Instead, most political leaders exploit the hatred between different religious groups (mainly the conflict between Hindus and Muslims) to secure their votes for the next electoral term. Gaining the vote of the Hindu majority gets easier for them by showing their support for creating a homogenous Hindu society in India.

Religion Fueling Genocides

"Most religions warn against war, yet more wars have been fought over religion than perhaps anything else."

- Mitch Albom

Ideological and institutionalized genocides have often stemmed from religious influences. Other ideologies, combined with the "Us vs. Them" mentality of extremism and justification through scripture, have been used in genocides of the past. Creating a utopian society of one religious group and eliminating all others is another ideological approach to committing genocide. On the other hand, institutionalized genocide has occurred in the expansion of military power and the dominating empires enforcing their religion upon the conquered states.

The persecution of Christians in the Roman Empire before Christianity was accepted as the official religion, the expulsion of

Muslims and Jews from Spain during the Inquisition, and the Rwandan genocide are all examples of how the state can use religion to target groups of people.

An argument in philosopher John K. Roth's paper on genocide and religious influences persuasively states that both ancient and modern genocide involves one or more of at least four factors or motivational drives: *'to eliminate a real or potential threat'*; *'to spread terror among real or potential enemies'*; *'to acquire economic wealth'*; or *'to implement a belief, a theory, or an ideology.'*[87]

Religion can be used as a driving force in three of the above factors. The most prominent is to spread the ideology (religion) by cultivating fear in the hearts of those who do not follow the same faith. It already covers the second factor mentioned by Roth, which can quickly progress to the complete elimination of the opponents upon retaliation or refusal to accept conversions.

In some cases, conversions also do not stop the genocide, as seen in the Bosnian genocide and the Holocaust. Thus, the religious identity of these people becomes similar to that of a racial identity, which cannot be altered by any means.

To the Nazis, a Jew who had accepted Christianity was still a Jew and deserved to be eliminated. The Serbian religious nationalism propagated that the Slavic Muslims suffered from a defective gene that could only be removed by eliminating them entirely. At the root of this aversion to the Bosniaks was the

[87] Roth, J. K. (2010). Easy to remember? Genocide and the philosophy of religion. International Journal for Philosophy of Religion, 1–3, 31–42. https://doi.org/10.1007/s11153-010-9256-3

ideology that in following the religion of the Turks, they would also kill the Serbs as the Turks had done so in the past. As a result, the Bosnian genocide occurred in which Bosniaks were murdered and expelled to cleanse the country of their existence.[88]

Othering, Justification, and Authorization

Othering is another concept that stems from the "Us vs. Them" mentality. The leaders of a particular religious group preach the superiority of their god and beliefs by portraying all other religious groups as inferior. In other cases, they can instill fear into the hearts of their believers that the other groups are their enemies and will kill them.[89]

This fusion of fear and hatred is dangerous in turning people against each other. As we already discussed in Chapter 4, it can lay the foundation for the "classification" of the different religious groups as the enemy/threat, which is the first stage of genocide. Thus, religious difference becomes the cause of hatred and later genocide.

However, othering is not the only factor that is used to manipulate people into committing genocide and other morally questionable acts for religion. It is the first step in differentiating the believers from the non-believers, then follows justification and authorization, which are equally as crucial for genocide committed under religious influences.

---

[88] Bartov, O., & Mack, P. (2001). In God's Name: Genocide and Religion in the Twentieth Century. Berghahn Books.

[89] Temoney, K. (2017). Religion and Genocide Nexuses: Bosnia as Case Study. Religions, 6, 112. https://doi.org/10.3390/rel8060112

Justification, as the word suggests, is to justify the heinous acts of killing, torture, and expulsion by using religious rhetoric and terminologies. The other group is dehumanized and alienized by portraying it as a threat to faith and religion, justifying why they had to be eliminated.

Lastly, authorization grants the power to perpetrators to carry out genocidal acts. Just like the Church was complicit in the Rwandan genocide and propagated a theology of genocide to eliminate the Tutsi, similarly, the Serbian Orthodox Church played a crucial role in the expulsion of the Bosniaks. Thus, these religious institutions not only justified genocide but also accepted the state authorizing it.[90]

Consider an example to understand this concept better. If a civilian kills his neighbor just for the reason that the victim associates with a different group, that behavior would be considered outlandish and worthy of punishment. However, if the reason behind killing that person is to eliminate a threat that would disrupt the cosmological order if not taken care of, then that act is regarded as a service to humanity and deemed honorable. That is how religious rhetoric can influence people into accepting deeds that are considered monstrous otherwise. Mass killings for the sake of power expansion might be frowned upon in many religions, but participating in a holy war to expand religious influence is seen as a remarkable feat worthy of being

---

[90] Schliesser, C. (2018). From "a Theology of Genocide" to a "Theology of Reconciliation"? On the Role of Christian Churches in the Nexus of Religion and Genocide in Rwanda. Religions, 2, 34. https://doi.org/10.3390/rel9020034

rewarded highly. In both instances, people are killed, but the reaction to the killings changes drastically.

Religion is misused to make people believe that they are doing the right thing by following the preaching of their religious or political leaders. By bringing the sensitive topic of faith into the argument, people are asked to give proof that they are true believers by subjecting them to the divine will. Thus, political and religious leaders can manipulate people into carrying out their hatred-infused plots by disguising them under the veil of faith and religion. Their faith could have been proved through honorable acts as well. Still, the teachings of always following the word of god and subjecting themselves to the powerful blindly caused them to get involved in genocide, mass murder, and other heinous deeds against other religious minorities.

As in the words of Dan Heist and Ram Cnaan: *"There are many ways by which people can actualize their faith. Hatred and terrorism is one way; serving people in need is another way."*[91]

It depends on how we choose; our faith can be shown through good deeds and spreading the message of peace. But in blindly following those who preach killing others and justify it with religious rhetoric, we are only defiling our faith with the blood of the people who suffer from the genocide and cruelty unleashed upon them.

Religion guides us on how to live life and who to worship, but making it a reason for eliminating other people due to fear or hatred is unacceptable by moral and most religious values.

---

[91] Heist, D., & Cnaan, R. (2016). Faith-Based International Development Work: A Review. Religions, 3, 19. https://doi.org/10.3390/rel7030019

Chapter 8: How Can the UN Stop Genocide?

"The United Nations is our one great hope for a peaceful and free world."

- *Ralph Bunche*

Genocide prevention is a topic that has been under debate ever since the term *'Genocide'* was coined in 1944 by Raphael Lemkin. Who should prevent genocide? Is it the collective responsibility of the world nations, or should there be a regulating authority imposing a framework or legislation to prevent genocide?

So far, the world's nations have looked to the United Nations to intervene and propose methods of prevention. The UN's mandate of Responsibility to Protect (R2P) and its existence as an unbiased organization for world peace makes it the best contender for preventing genocide.

Ten years after the Rwandan Genocide, UN Secretary-General Kofi Annan presented a five-point action plan for the prevention of genocide. This action plan included preventing armed conflict, protecting civilians in armed conflict, ending impunity through judicial action, setting up an early warning system on the basis of gathered information, and taking swift and decisive action to stop genocide.[92]

---

[92] UN Action Plan to Prevent Genocide (Kofi Annan, April 7, 2004) - - Prevent Genocide International. (n.d.). Prevent Genocide International.

According to this action plan, the UN has the power to stop genocide by even taking military action if the need arises. However, current challenges and limitations only result in the UN imposing sanctions without any decisive action.

In this chapter, we will discuss the role of the United Nations in preventing genocide, the existing mechanism, challenges and limitations, and the suggestions for action required in order to avoid genocide.

UN's Role in Preventing Genocide

"Preventing genocide is a collective obligation. Let us continue to work together to ensure a future forever free of genocide."

- Ban Ki-moon

The role of the United Nations is to keep peace in the world and prevent any situation that might lead to World War III. Before the formation of the UN, the League of Nations existed as an organizing body over multiple nation-states. However, it was abolished at the start of World War II as it failed in its fundamental purpose of preventing war. As a result, the United Nations was established in 1946 to maintain peace in the world and prevent war.

After the Second World War, genocide was recognized as a mass atrocity, so its prevention also fell under the umbrella of preventing war crimes, atrocities, and crimes against humanity. With over 190 members, the UN is the sole organizing body that

---

http://www.preventgenocide.org/prevent/UNdocs/KofiAnnansActionPlantoPreventGenocide7Apr2004.htm

can spread a global message and stop these crimes by bringing them into the spotlight. Under Secretary-General Kofi Annan, an action plan was passed to prevent genocide consisting of these five points:

1. Preventing armed conflict: Most genocides have occurred during wars, so the key point is to prevent armed conflicts. Whether it is a conflict between two countries or within the populations of a country, armed conflict can cause the unrest to escalate to genocide and other crimes against humanity. The UN supports the national efforts of the countries to stop armed conflicts and also provides aid and awareness to prevent them.

2. Protecting civilians in armed conflict: As part of the UN's mandate and the Responsibility to Protect, the organization ensures the protection of civilian lives during armed conflicts taking place anywhere in the world. Humanitarian aid, safe shelters, and other facilitation are often provided by the UN to civilians. However, most of these civilians attain the status of refugees after the conflict ends, as there are no other preventive measures to restore their property, security, and national identity.

3. Ending impunity through judicial action: Generally, crime is only prevented when there is a proper punishment. If states suffering from genocide or other mass atrocities are unable to punish the perpetrators, the independent tribunal of the International Criminal Court can investigate the case and take action on their behalf. Its primary role is to conduct trials for genocide, war crimes, and other crimes against humanity. It follows the International humanitarian law and indicts people for violating it.[93]

4. Gathering information and setting up early warning systems: After the tragedies of Rwanda and the Balkans in the 1990s, special advisors were appointed by the UN Secretary-General in 2004. These advisors on the departments of the Prevention of Genocide and the Responsibility to Protect gathered information on the countries at risk of genocide, war crimes, ethnic cleansing, and crimes against humanity. They are then tasked to bring these situations to the attention of the Secretary-General, who can present the issue to the Security Council and decide to take action.

Another approach taken by the UN is "nowcasting," which refers to predicting the present along with looking at future outcomes and past causes. In places that are at risk of genocide, early warning systems (such as crime risk assessment models and forecasting) are set to alert the organization to take timely action against the perpetrators. Emerging violent action can be countered effectively through these violent actions, thus preventing its escalation to genocide.[94]

5. Taking swift and decisive action: According to this action plan, swift and decisive action could also include military action. When all other methods of establishing peace and preventing

---

[93] UN Action Plan to Prevent Genocide (Kofi Annan, April 7, 2004) - - Prevent Genocide International. (n.d.). Prevent Genocide International. Retrieved May 3, 2024, from http://www.preventgenocide.org/prevent/UNdocs/KofiAnnansActionPlantoPreventGenocide7Apr2004.htm

[94] Heldt, B. (2018). Statistical Approach to early detection. In B. Harff & T. R. Gurr, Preventing Mass Atrocities. Routledge.

genocide fail, military action should be taken by the UN against the perpetrators. However, this point doesn't specify who will take military action on behalf of the UN as it doesn't have an army of its own. Although international coalitions can be called up to prevent genocide through military action, the only such instance seen in history was to stop the killings in Libya under the Qadhafi regime.[95]

However, this action plan could not be implemented completely, as seen in the case of the recent genocide taking place in Palestine. The challenges and limitations that might restrict this action plan in the current scenario are also discussed in the chapter.

Aside from these five points, there are other ways the UN can play its role as a peacekeeping organization. It can implement measures of preventive justice, protect the national sovereignty of each state no matter how big or small, and pass UN reforms. The UN personnel should commit to their roles morally and ethically, ensuring that no political or individual benefits stop them from making the right decision. Wherever there is a risk of violence, the UN should make proper intervention through reforms and resolutions as well as action if needed.[96]

---

[95] UN Action Plan to Prevent Genocide (Kofi Annan, April 7, 2004) - - Prevent Genocide International. (n.d.). Prevent Genocide International. Retrieved May 3, 2024, from http://www.preventgenocide.org/prevent/UNdocs/KofiAnnansActionPlantoPreventGenocide7Apr2004.htm

[96] Kamanzi, S. (2004). PREVENTING GENOCIDE: THE ROLE OF THE UNITED NATIONS. ILSA Journal of International & Comparative Law. https://core.ac.uk/download/pdf/51096646.pdf

Existing Mechanisms for Genocide Prevention

"If the United Nations once admits that international disputes can be settled by using force, then we will have destroyed the foundation of the organization and our best hope of establishing a world order."

- Dwight D. Eisenhower

The United Nations is a peace-ensuring organization, and as a result, all its mechanisms focus on stopping armed conflict and establishing peace. Therefore, it doesn't take military action against countries or groups involved in armed conflict, as the situation can escalate to a full-fledged war. In cases of genocide, the Genocide Convention of 1948 is referred to, but even that document does not mention any judicial process that could be implemented to prevent genocide. As a result, the responsibility falls solely on the UN as a global peace organization with memberships from most world nations to prevent genocide.[97]

The UN has designated departments and independent bodies to deal with the international problems of war crimes and mass atrocities. It has helped nations heal from the horrible aftermath of war and genocide, providing humanitarian aid, assisting refugees to seek political asylum in other member states, and ensuring civilians' safety in times of crisis. However, it still lacks a direct intervention approach, which was clearly seen in the case of the Rwandan Genocide in 1994. Even though it has worked considerably to support the Rwandan minorities years later, direct intervention and not withdrawing their troops from

[97] Bauer, Y. (2018). Genocide and mass atrocities. In Preventing Mass Atrocities (pp. 11–24). Routledge. http://dx.doi.org/10.4324/9781315665931-2

Rwanda in 1994 could have prevented such mass destruction and loss of human lives.[98]

The responsibilities and the roles these UN bodies play in ensuring peace are discussed below:

Security Council: The Security Council is the most important organ of the United Nations that can take action to stop genocide. It consists of 15 members, out of which five are permanent (USA, Russia, China, France, and UK), whereas the other members are elected for a two-year mandate. The Security Council is responsible for making all the decisions that form the backbone of the UN and also works to maintain peace and security in the world.[99]

For any decision to be approved, all permanent members have to agree on it. The decision cannot be implemented if even one nation uses the veto power. This has been the case for several genocides in the past, as one or two permanent members used their veto for political reasons. The Security Council has only taken action in rare cases, such as that of Kenya in 2007-2008, Macedonia in 2001, and Timor Leste in 2007, to stop genocide and protect civilian lives.[100]

---

[98] Haller, T. (2020). "The Role of the United Nations in the Prevention of Genocide." Honors Theses. 78. https://digitalcommons.assumption.edu/honorstheses/78

[99] Schabas, W. A. (2006). Preventing Genocide and Mass Killing: The Challenge for the United Nations - Minority Rights Group. Minority Rights Group. https://minorityrights.org/resources/preventing-genocide-and-mass-killing-the-challenge-for-the-united-nations/

[100] Bauer, Y. (2018). Genocide and mass atrocities. In Preventing Mass Atrocities (pp. 11–24). Routledge. http://dx.doi.org/10.4324/9781315665931-2

General Assembly: As the UN's representative organ, it is the platform for all the member nations to present their perspectives and participate in discussions. The General Assembly also adopted the Genocide Convention in 1948 in its third session. However, the General Assembly does not have the power to take any substantial action on cases of genocide, mass violence, armed conflicts, and other war crimes. Its broad representation gives it the credibility to present resolutions based on the discussion occurring among the member states. Thus, it serves as a global microphone to broadcast the views of all member states on current and prevailing issues of genocide and violations of human rights.[101]

In the ongoing genocide of Palestinians, the General Assembly played the role of an unbiased global platform that allowed the nations to speak out on the issue and call for a ceasefire.

Secretariat: The Secretariat is the office of the Chief Administrative Officer of the UN, the Secretary-General. It collaborates closely with the Security Council and the General Assembly, feeding information to the organ responsible for decision-making. Its special advisors on Genocide Prevention and Responsibility to Protect investigate the potential cases of genocide or mass atrocities and report to the Security Council. Any action by the Security Council is based on the decisions made by the Secretary-General. Thus, this position faces the credit for all successful interventions and is also blamed for the UN's failures.

---

[101] Schabas, W. A. (2006). Preventing Genocide and Mass Killing: The Challenge for the United Nations - Minority Rights Group. Minority Rights Group. https://minorityrights.org/resources/preventing-genocide-and-mass-killing-the-challenge-for-the-united-nations/

International Court of Justice: The International Court of Justice is the primary judicial organ of the United Nations and holds the responsibility of settling disputes between nations and upholding the International legal system. It is composed of 15 judges elected by the General Assembly who oversee cases submitted to the court where international intervention is required. The judgments passed by the ICJ cannot be changed and are binding on the involved parties. It can also issue advisory opinions on legal questions referred by authorized UN organs and specialized agencies.

These UN organs help the organization keep track of the situation of peace in the world and stop emerging conflicts through early intervention. The UN also works to build the resilience of societies against such crimes by ensuring the rule of law and protecting human rights without discrimination.

Challenges and Limitations

"The United Nations must focus on delivery rather than process and on people rather than bureaucracy."

- Antonio Guterres

The United Nations primarily follows International humanitarian law, and its decisions are based on this foundation. However, International humanitarian law does not directly address the source of armed conflict. As a result, the UN, despite intervening, has to take an unbiased and neutral approach. This sometimes gives more power to the perpetrators to carry out the offenses of mass killing and genocide in secret, as seen in the killing fields of the Khmer Rouge's regime in Cambodia.[102]

The UN's diplomatic approach to solving matters is also a big challenge that limits it from taking action. In maintaining peace and not resorting to armed conflict, the organization passes resolutions and threatens the perpetrators with sanctions. However, these diplomatic efforts only delay the prevention of genocide and other war crimes, leading to more deaths. The genocide taking place in East Timor was an example of the devastating aftermath of this diplomatic approach. For many years, the UN tried to solve the issue diplomatically, which led to further killing and mass atrocities. The resolutions passed on Indonesia by the UN were ignored; still, no definite action was taken against the state.[103]

Therefore, the UN's biggest challenges and limitations are its status as an unbiased global platform, its approach to solving matters diplomatically, and its refraining from military action in fear of causing another global war. However, we can not ignore the significance of the UN as a global peacekeeping organization. It can still play an influential role in preventing genocide and helping the victims recover from the aftermath. A few suggestions on how the UN can expand its role and facilitate the victims of genocide are discussed below.

---

[102] Schabas, W. A. (2006). Preventing Genocide and Mass Killing: The Challenge for the United Nations - Minority Rights Group. Minority Rights Group. https://minorityrights.org/resources/preventing-genocide-and-mass-killing-the-challenge-for-the-united-nations/

[103] Totten, S., & Bartrop, P. R. (2004). The United Nations and genocide: Prevention, intervention, and prosecution. Human Rights Review, 4, 8–31. https://doi.org/10.1007/s12142-004-1025-1

Suggestion 1: Uniform Global Constitution

"The purpose of the United Nations should be to protect the essential sovereignty of nations, large and small."

- Nikita Khrushchev

The term Uniform Global Constitution refers to a constitution formed by the United Nations that is applicable to all member countries. As a result, 193 countries of the world would follow a uniform set of legislation that would make it easier to prevent crime and punish. In cases of genocide, such as Bosnia and Darfur, the main reason why the UN couldn't intervene to a larger extent was the differences in the constitution and legislation of each country. However, if all members follow a Uniform Global Constitution, such a situation would not arise.

A uniform constitution would ensure that the same laws are enforced in all countries, the legal system is constant, and the punishments for all criminal offenses are also constant. For genocide committed in any part of the world, the punishment would be the same. Thus, the UN will have the power to take action against the perpetrators and protect the people, preventing genocide effectively.

Suggestion 2: UN Citizenship for Refugees

"More than ever before in human history, we share a common destiny. We can master it only if we face it together. And that, my friends, is why we have the United Nations."

- Kofi Annan

A large number of people are driven out of their homes and forced to become refugees due to genocides. They have no citizenship, and even their fundamental rights are compromised. Staying in their native lands becomes impossible due to the crimes they have faced and the uncertainties in their future.

As a result, they are left homeless and stateless, forced to take refuge in other countries.

Legal documentation should exist for these refugees to counter this issue, along with the prevention of genocide, granting them the power to relocate to a state and start their lives afresh. The UN can establish citizenship for refugees to be recognized as citizens of the United Nations.

All their legal documents, including their passport, can fall under the domain of the UN, allowing them to travel between the member states freely and live in member states without compromising their fundamental rights. Proper education, shelter, and healthcare would all be accessible to them as citizens of the UN.

In conclusion, the United Nations has great potential to be used as a global platform with sufficient power to stop genocide. If the current challenges and limitations are overcome and all members come together on the same page of global peace and harmony, then such acts posing risks to innocent civilians can be stopped effectively.

The UN's lack of intervention in the past and the destruction it led to can serve as a learning outcome for them to modify their existing mechanism and take action where human rights are being violated, especially in cases where genocide and mass atrocities are taking place.

The recent ongoing genocide of Palestine can become the starting point for the UN to do more than just provide humanitarian aid to the victims.

Chapter 9: What Can YOU Do?

"It is in the power of every individual to do that which the community as a whole is powerless to effect."

- *William Thomas Stead*

The world said 'Never Again' after the Holocaust when the Genocide Convention was passed. However, the previous century showed that genocides continued to occur and are going on even today, as in the case of the Palestinian Genocide, the Ughyur Muslims Genocide, and the Rohingya Genocide.

Where do we stand as an international community advocating for peace when we don't take any measures to prevent genocide ourselves? It is a state of utter shame that most of us refuse to act against the atrocities affecting humanity. Instead of constantly looking up at global organizations like the UN, it is our responsibility to protect those in need too on the individual and collective level.

Most people refuse to act individually, which in turn deprives society of a vast number of people who could have come together to take a stand for the right cause. Don't think you can't do anything because you are just one person. There are many who feel this way instead of coming together to form a collective force against injustice. YOU create the masses, and as a result, YOU have the power to stop genocide.

Early Warning Signs

To prevent genocide, we must be aware of the early warning signs of an emerging conflict that can escalate to the horrific level of genocide and mass atrocity. Some common findings while researching the cases of different genocides showed that all these conflicts depicted early warning signs that were ignored by the state and other authorities.

Most genocides of the twentieth century could have been prevented if necessary action had been taken in the earlier stages when the genocide-prone behavior started to show. However, the international community delayed speaking up at the right time, which led to the genocide taking place.[104]

Some of the early warning signs that shouldn't be ignored are discussed below:

Tension and polarization: The first sign of potentially violent conflicts is tension and polarization between the groups involved. This is also referred to as the 'Us vs. Them' mentality, where two groups are pitted against each other due to their differences. The social, racial, ethnic, religious, or ideological differences of certain groups often result in polarization, as seen in the case of the Rwandan Genocide in 1994, where the people polarized into the Tutsi and Hutu groups, and tension increased among them. The recent case of the Israel and Palestine conflict also arose from the tension and polarization between the Arab natives and the Jewish settlers in 1948.[105]

Apocalyptic public rhetoric: This term refers to the claims made by certain groups that the other groups would destroy

---

[104] Hamburg, D. A. (2015). Preventing Genocide: Practical Steps Toward Early Detection and Effective Action. Routledge.

[105] Straus, S. (2016). Fundamentals of Genocide and Mass Atrocity Prevention. United States Holocaust Memorial Museum.

them or, in other words, cause an apocalyptic situation. The masses are often steered to genocide using the notion of '*destroy them to save us*,' as seen in the case of the Holocaust, where the general public was led to believe that the Jews were a threat to the society and their religion, thus justifying the reason for their eradication.[106]

Labeling civilian groups as the enemy: Often, the state or other authorities might label a certain civilian group as the enemy and drive the masses to revolt against them. Examples include the Holocaust, the Rohingya Muslim Genocide, and the Armenian Genocide. Recently, in the ongoing genocide of the Palestinians, Israeli authorities have labeled the Palestinian civilians complicit with Hamas, thus portraying them as the enemy of the state of Israel.

Development/deployment of irregular armed forces: Another warning sign is the increased employment of armed groups that can be used to attack civilians under the name of the state. Hitler's rearmament of German troops, which broke the Treaty of Versailles, was an early warning sign of the upcoming Holocaust. However, the allied states ignored that warning which led to the genocide of European Jews at the hands of the Nazis.[107]

Stockpiling weapons: Accumulation of weaponry is also an alarming factor and should not go unnoticed by the respective

---

[106] Straus, S. (2012). "Destroy Them to Save Us": Theories of Genocide and the Logics of Political Violence. Terrorism and Political Violence, 4, 544–560. https://doi.org/10.1080/09546553.2012.700611

[107] Ranke, J. (2011). The Anglo-American Press and the 'Secret' Rearmament of Hitler's Germany, 1933 to 1935. All Theses. 1259. https://tigerprints.clemson.edu/all_theses/1259

authorities. These weapons include but are not limited to explosives, handguns, assault rifles, mines, and grenades—or any other weapon that could effectively harm civilians. As these weapons can later be used to commit mass atrocities and cause destruction, it is safer to put a stop to their stockpiling in time. If a state or a particular group is accumulating weapons for no justifiable reason, it should be answerable in international courts if the matter can not be resolved by their national governments. Aside from the reason for weapon accumulation, it is also important to note how the weapons are distributed. If they are distributed to groups already polarized against each other, it is like adding fuel to fire.[108]

Emergency or discriminatory legislation: In cases where the state is targeting certain minorities, emergency laws and regulations are created to oppress the minority groups further. If these emergency laws are clearly discriminatory and not in accordance with International humanitarian law, then it can be considered an early warning sign of genocide. Such laws exploit the rights of minorities, and action should be taken in time to stop the situation from worsening. The Nuremberg laws enforced in Nazi Germany are a clear example of how legislation can be used to discriminate and oppress a particular group of people. This is also an example of the fifth stage of genocide, in which the perpetrators use organized methods to get rid of the other group.

---

[108] Straus, S. (2016). Fundamentals of Genocide and Mass Atrocity Prevention. United States Holocaust Memorial Museum.

Removing moderates from leadership or public service: The term *Moderates* refers to people in leadership who take a moderate approach while dealing with polarized groups. Instead of taking hard action, they try to seek a diplomatic way out that tries to solve the issue without needing any armed conflict. When these moderates are silenced and removed from power, leaving only the hard and fast actors in charge, conflicts get worse and often result in mass atrocities.

Impunity for past crimes: If past acts of violence or oppression against a certain group go unpunished and the perpetrators are not held accountable for their actions, it may embolden them to commit atrocities at a large scale. Four years before the Rwandan Genocide, Tutsi civilians were killed in a series of attacks that went unpunished by the authorities. Even though not all small-scale acts of violence escalate to the vast proportion of genocide, if those small-scale acts are unaccounted for, then it paves the path for more violence, as seen in Rwanda. Four years later, the Hutu struck again and committed genocide that resulted in mass destruction and loss of life for the Tutsi minority.

These warning signs indicate that the state or region is at risk of genocide. As a responsible global community, we should raise our voices to nip the evil in the bud and stop the conflict before it takes its toll.

Aside from the warning signs, the triggers of genocide and mass atrocity should also be taken notice of. These triggers include high-level assassinations, coups or attempted coups, changes in conflict dynamics, crackdowns on protests, and symbolically significant attacks against individuals or physical sites.[109]

Signs of Change

There are three main ways to bring change that can have a practical impact and prevent crimes like genocide. These ways were labeled as the Pro-civilian strategy of bringing change by conviction, coercion, and incentive.

Conviction: Pro-civilian arguments are to convince authorities against genocide and other crimes targeting innocent citizens. These include moral arguments on the topics of innocence of citizens, self-preservation, respecting civilian obligations, and the preciousness and vulnerability of human life. Conviction is often the first step in bringing any change or putting an end to any unpleasant event.

Coercion: If the step of conviction fails or yields no effective result, the second step is coercion. Pro-civilian coercions include peaceful protests, political pressure, economic pressure through boycotts, and maintaining pro-civilian authority. The state can be challenged to reconsider its decisions and policies if a majority of its people are unhappy with the results and convey it through protests and other mass movements.

Incentive: Another sign of change is to bring incentives and rewards that can yield positive results. Rewards of peace and

---

[109] Straus, S. (2016). Fundamentals of Genocide and Mass Atrocity Prevention. United States Holocaust Memorial Museum.

good conduct can encourage a positive image, preventing the perpetrators from having to resort to genocide.

However, these three signs are suggestions that can be implemented to bring change. Their effectiveness in preventing crimes and mass atrocities depends on the people who are involved, the perpetrators who are being addressed, and an array of other political and ideological factors. Mentioning them before the measures was important as the individual and collective measures you can take as a member of a responsible international community stems from these three signs of change.[110]

Measures to Stop Genocide

"Preventing genocide is a collective and individual responsibility."

- *Ban Ki-Moon*

The above quote by former Secretary-General Ban Ki-Moon emphasizes that we should take measures to prevent genocide as it is our individual and collective responsibility.

However, what can we do in such a fragile situation?

How can we act to stop genocide?

These questions often silence the young voices that are raised against this atrocity, but it is high time for us to understand the

---

[110] Slim, H., & Mancini-Griffoli, D. (2008). Interpreting violence: anti-civilian thinking and practice and how to argue against it more effectively | HD. Center for Humanitarian Dialogue. https://hdcentre.org/insights/interpreting-violence-anti-civilian-thinking-and-practice-and-how-to-argue-against-it-more-effectively/

role we play in the international community and wield our power against genocide.

On an individual and collective level, you can take the following measures to stop genocide:

Educate yourself: The first step is to educate yourself and become aware of the different types of genocide, the causes and reasons behind them, the destruction they caused, and how they could be prevented. You can find hundreds of resources on the Internet, including books, articles, research papers, and news that you can use to gain awareness about genocides and form your unbiased view.[111]

Spread awareness: Once you have all the information, it is your responsibility to spread awareness and educate others on their responsibility to raise their voices for oppressed communities. Spreading awareness adds people to the cause and elevates your individual efforts to a collective level that can have a larger impact.

Shaping pro-civilian dialogue: raising your voice for the speechless, the people who cannot fight back or take a stand for themselves, helps shape a pro-civilian dialogue. At its very origin, genocide is an anti-civilian movement that endangers the lives of innocents and destroys multiple generations. Civilian lives belonging to any group, race, social class, ethnicity, religion, etc, are of utmost significance and should be protected. This can only

---

[111] O'Connor, T. (2023). How to Stop Genocide and Prevent Atrocities. Everyday Peacebuilding. https://everydaypeacebuilding.com/how-to-end-genocide-and-prevent-atrocities/

be possible if the civilians take a stand for each other and create healthy dialogue between groups to unite them.[112]

Peaceful protests: If merely creating a dialogue between the feuding groups is not enough, or if authoritative figures and the state are involved in committing genocide, then the public and the international community can force them to stop through peaceful protests and raising their voices against injustice on a global level.

Mobilizing mass movements: Similar to peaceful protests, mass movements can be mobilized to create pressure on the perpetrators and force the authorities into taking action against them. These mass movements are not just confined to a specific region; they are only effective when the majority of mankind is involved, without being restricted by national or ethnocentric boundaries. They stand for the common grounds of humanity.

Mobilizing policymakers: Similar to a chain reaction, all the steps you take on individual and collective levels come together to have a deeper impact. Mass movements can drive policymakers to take note of the situation and create legislation that condemns violence and punishes the perpetrators. According to Gregory H. Stanton, we are all capable of evil and must be restrained by law from committing it. Therefore, it is our collective responsibility to highlight the issue of genocide and

---

[112] Slim, H., & Mancini-Griffoli, D. (2008). Interpreting violence: anti-civilian thinking and practice and how to argue against it more effectively | HD. Center for Humanitarian Dialogue. https://hdcentre.org/insights/interpreting-violence-anti-civilian-thinking-and-practice-and-how-to-argue-against-it-more-effectively/

other crimes against humanity to the extent that proper laws are made for dealing with them.[113]

Humanitarian aid: Contributing to sending humanitarian aid to the people suffering from genocide and armed conflicts, reduced to the status of refugees, or displaced from their homelands is also our collective responsibility. You can donate to humanitarian organizations working in those areas to provide relief to the victims.

These are some of the ways you can contribute to preventing genocide. However, the discourse doesn't stop at just these points; it depends on how you fulfill your responsibility. The more part you play for the protection of innocent people, the more impact your efforts will have.

The Palestinian Genocide — Global Efforts

The global efforts by the international community to stop the ongoing Palestinian Genocide show the measures taken by civilians, students, and policymakers to call for a ceasefire and stop the state of Israel from further oppressing the native Palestinians.

Some of the notable efforts that have been made at individual and collective levels, showing the power of mankind standing up against genocide, are mentioned below:

---

[113] Stanton, G. H. (2003). Commentary: How We Can Prevent Genocide. University of Hawaii System; Genocide Watch. https://www.hawaii.edu/powerkills/COMM.6.24.03.HTM

- Protests for a ceasefire took place in major cities worldwide. People called for a ceasefire and Palestine's liberation in the public squares and streets of London, New York, Madrid, and Istanbul. Malaysian citizens gathered around the US embassy on the Global Day of Action for Gaza, calling for a ceasefire. In Johannesburg, South Africa, protestors gathered around the US consulate in protest against the genocide, accusing the US of being complicit in the act due to its support of Israel.[114]

- Students form a vast population standing up for human rights and a ceasefire in Palestine. Countless protests were held by university students defying their institutions' attempts to silence them, as seen recently in the renaming of Columbia University's Hamilton Hall to Hind's Hall after a six-year-old girl who died in Palestine.[115]

- Million's worth of humanitarian aid was sent from all over the world to the refugees in Gaza, Rafah, and other affected cities of Palestine.

- Countries such as South Africa, Ireland, Norway, Algeria, Brazil, and many more protested against Israel's continuous bombing of hospitals and civilian settlements. They presented

---

[114] Pro-Palestine protests held around the world as Gaza war nears 100 days | Israel War on Gaza News | Al Jazeera. (2024). Al Jazeera. https://www.aljazeera.com/news/2024/1/13/pro-palestine-demonstrations-around-the-world-as-gaza-war-nears-100-days

[115] Watkins, A. (2024). Columbia Protesters Rename Hamilton Hall to 'Hind's Hall.' The New York Times. https://www.nytimes.com/2024/04/30/nyregion/columbia-protesters-hind-rajab-hamilton-hall.html

their perspective on stopping genocide in the addresses held in the United Nations General Assembly.

These efforts and more are currently ongoing, mobilizing the world to prevent genocide and ensure peace and harmony for all.

Never Again can only become a reality if we are all united to make it possible and play our part in preventing genocide.

Chapter 10: Beware of Different Forms of Genocide

"Together, we can prevent genocide from happening again. Together, we can make a better future for our children."

- Dith Pran

To prevent genocide, we must all understand the reasons that lead to it, the early warning signs, and the different forms of genocide. No action can be taken based on ignorance; being aware and knowing how to act is our greatest defense against this heinous crime.

Preventing a crime that has such deep roots and an impact that extends globally as all humanity witnesses its horrors requires an effective strategy, which cannot be possible without complete awareness. By being aware, we can take the right action, recognize genocide, and contribute to the efforts to stop it.

Therefore, this chapter will discuss the different forms of genocide that have occurred throughout world history and also elaborate on further strategies for genocide prevention.

Forms of Genocide

"Every genocide starts with words of hatred and ends with mass killings."

- Samantha Power

Genocide has taken different forms throughout history, and we can not measure each one of them up to the Holocaust. True, the Holocaust is an unforgettable genocide that took place during World War II, through which this term became recognized, and the crime was deemed punishable in international courts. But we have to acknowledge that to label a conflict as genocide, we don't have to wait for the atrocities to reach the extent of Nazi Germany's level.

Thus, the different forms of genocide are discussed below so that you can be aware of them and prevent them effectively:

Retributive Genocide: Even though retribution plays a role in almost all genocides, it becomes a rationalization in this form (blaming the victim for the cause of mass extermination). Perpetrators of this form of genocide blame one group for being the root cause of all problems and consider the only solution that could bring peace is wiping that group out. Retributive Genocide occurred in the conquests led by Genghis Khan, who proclaimed that the people he subjected to mass killing were responsible for their own demise. Vengeance was a key motivator for him to inflict genocide upon the masses of the regions he conquered.[116]

Institutional Genocide: This form of genocide is the politically sanctioned mass murder, examples of which took place in ancient and medieval times. As conquests occurred on a global scale, the mass murder and enslavement of the natives became common. Institutional genocide is organized, the perpetrators are armed and trained, and institutions exist to prepare them for the mass killing. As a result, the destruction caused by these genocides is much higher. It is motivated by a desire to show

---

[116] Grousset, R. (1972). Conqueror of the World: The Life of Chingis-Khan (M. McKellar & D. Sinor, Trans.). Viking Press.

power through violence, claiming land and resources by force and removing the possibility of retaliation by killing the indigenous people. All genocides that took place in conquests can be categorized as institutional genocide.[117]

Utilitarian Genocide: Utility has played a significant role in institutional genocides, but in the sixteenth and nineteenth centuries, it became a form of genocide itself. The genocides of the indigenous people of Africa, Australia, the Americas, India, and Tasmania are examples of utilitarian genocide in which organized groups seized power, wiped out the natives, and then exploited the resources. Genocidal attacks in the name of progress and development and eliminating some people so that others can live well are characteristic indicators of utilitarian genocide. Other theories that give rise to this form of genocide are attempts to curtail the surplus population resulting from rapid development, as argued by Richard Rubenstein. Thus, utilitarian genocide can occur against natives of a region that has been taken over by external invaders/conquerors or against minority groups in an already prospering region.[118]

Monopolistic Genocide: A genocide that occurs domestically in a state for the monopolization of power is called monopolistic genocide. Most of the genocides after the twentieth century were internalized in different states, thus rightfully called monopolistic. Examples include the Armenian Genocide, the Cambodian Genocide, and the Bangladeshi (East Pakistan) Genocide. These genocides have two main factors in common;

---

[117] Walker, T. A. (1899). A History of the Law of Nations. Cambridge University Press.
[118] Rubenstein, R. L. (1983). The Age of Triage: Fear and Hope in an Overcrowded World. Boston: Beacon Press.

first, they occurred within the same state, and second, they were enforced by political regimes wanting to establish their rule and monopoly.[119]

Ideological Genocide: Genocide fueled by an ideology takes the form of ideological genocide. Religion is also an ideology; thus, all religious genocides are examples of ideological genocide. The Holocaust itself was an ideological genocide, targeted toward a specific religious group (Jews) and led by Hitler's ideology of cleansing Europe of all Jews. Albert Camus labels it as a metaphysical revolt against the conditions of human existence. He defines it as an attempt at recreation and purification of society by wiping out a particular group and using strong ideology to rally the masses against them.[120]

By calling Jews the robbers of Christianity and a threat to mankind, Nazi Germany was able to continue with the horrors of the Holocaust. Using religion and ideology to cause acts of human destructiveness is common throughout world history, as there are several other cases of ideological genocide, such as the Rohingya Muslim Genocide, the Bosnian Genocide, as well as the ongoing Palestinian Genocide. The state of Israel uses the ideology of *'Promised Homeland'* to force the indigenous Palestinians out of their land and subject them to mass killing, torture, and extermination.

History is full of genocidal accounts occurring from as far back as Prehistoric times to the detailed records of conquests by

---

[119] Smith, R. W. (2000). Genocide and the Modern Age (pp. 21–36). Syracuse University Press.
[120] Camus, A. (1956). The Rebel (A. Bower, Trans.). Vintage Books.

Assyrians, Greeks, Romans, the Crusaders, the Mongols, the Spaniards, and so on. These different forms of genocide have occurred in various regions of the world, and now, as responsible human beings, we must recognize them and devise ways to stop them.

Ethnocide vs. Genocide

The term *'Ethnocide'* refers to the killing of a culture or way of living without killing its bearers. In other words, it is the destruction of indigenous people's cultural way of life by forcing them to adopt another culture. Practicing their culture and language becomes forbidden and sometimes declared a punishable offense.[121]

Ethnocide is different from genocide because, in this case, people are not killed or forced out of their homes primarily. Retaliations are met with severe action from influential groups, but killing people is not the main objective of the perpetrators. Commonly, it is known as cultural genocide, and the ethnocide of Catalonians is an example of this crime.

However, ethnocide can evolve into ethnic cleansing if the oppressed groups retaliate and the hatred against them increases. Ethnic cleansing, as discussed previously, is the wiping out of a particular ethnicity to create a homogenous society. The conflicts between Spain and Catalonia led to massacres, which

---

[121] Totten, S., Parsons, W. S., & Hitchcock, R. K. (2002). Confronting Genocide and Ethnocide of Indigenous Peoples: An Interdisciplinary Approach to Definition, Intervention, Prevention, and Advocacy. In A. L. Hinton, Annihilating Difference: The Anthropology of Genocide (pp. 54–92). University of California Press. http://dx.doi.org/10.1525/california/9780520230286.003.0003

are an example of ethnic cleansing (killing people or expulsing them from their native land based on their ethnicity). Catalonians were killed and imprisoned in General Franco's regime, and their cultural heritage was destroyed.[122]

These different typologies of ethnocide, genocide, politicide (annihilation of political movements and their members), and democide (murder or mass murder organized by the state) are used to further specify what type of mass atrocities are taking place. However, the confusion around these terms causes delays in proper action and intervention.

Further Strategies for Prevention

Learning from the lessons of the past, the following strategies for genocide prevention should be implemented on a large scale to stop genocide and create an example out of the perpetrators such that the crime does not repeat:

Proactive Help (Preventive Diplomacy): Permanent mechanisms should be implemented worldwide for settling conflicts before they become a crisis. Recognize dangers early through warning signs and foster a widespread public understanding of conflict resolution and violence prevention. Support moderate and pragmatic leaders to work as democratic reformers and solve the issues arising within a state before they take the form of genocide or other crimes against humanity. Early detection and mediation are also essential tools of preventive diplomacy.

---

[122] Vilanova, F. (2017). Did Catalonia endure a (cultural) genocide? Journal of Catalan Intellectual History, 11, 15–32. https://doi.org/10.1515/jocih-2016-0002

Fostering Worldwide Democracy: Dictatorships are prone to genocide as all the control is in the hands of one influential person or political group. Therefore, the system of democracy should be promoted worldwide, and a union of these democratic states can be used to further inhibit the risks of genocide. A global organization of democracies can prevent violence and armed conflicts by setting standards for fair and free elections, providing guidance for education at all levels, and using the institutions of the state to mobilize intellectual and moral leadership.

Fostering Equitable Socioeconomic Development: The risk of war and genocide can also be reduced by fostering socioeconomic development worldwide. According to David A. Hamburg, socioeconomic development links with democracy as crucial ingredients for genocide prevention. Through this strategy, democracies of the world can be empowered by providing them with features essential for socioeconomic development (knowledge, skills, freedom, and health). The more established and developed democracies can come together to firmly ground new democracies and help them on their road to development through training, education, and support in terms of health and welfare. Once these systems and infrastructure are up and running, the new or underdeveloped democratic states will also be able to achieve a sound socioeconomic status.

Education for Human Survival: Comprehensive education that is accessible to all citizens is a significant tool for human survival and collective development. Therefore, the schools become the learning grounds for advancing science and technology, promoting holistic societies, eradicating hatred, and fostering brotherhood among all, regardless of race, gender, religion, ethnicity, etc. Instead of denying the existence and harmful impact of genocide, the youth should be allowed to learn about it fully and engage in constructive discussions where they realize that hatred and elimination are never the solution.

Use of International Justice: Human rights abuse and mass violence lead to genocide and cause conflicts that threaten the stability of a region. If the state finds it difficult to control these factors, international justice can be used as a means of prevention and intervention. Cooperating democracies and international organizations such as the ICJ and the ICC can play their role in recognizing the conflicts and stopping them by holding the perpetrators responsible according to International humanitarian law.

Restraints on Highly Lethal Weapons: Accumulation of highly lethal weapons within a state by a particular group should be viewed as an early warning sign. If no action is taken, it can lead to that group using its power against a minority and initiating genocide. Proper laws should be devised to forbid the misuse of weapons and restrict them only for the state's defensive purposes. Global cooperation between states can further help avoid external conflicts as stronger states could provide security assistance to weaker states.

By being alert, thoroughly informed, organizationally prepared, and morally committed, we can stop genocide and social injustice before it becomes a major issue and cause of destruction. Our role as a cooperative international community is necessary for safeguarding human rights worldwide.[123]

Bearing Witness

"For the dead and the living, we must bear witness."

- Elie Wiesel

Our ancestors bore witness to these genocides, and now we are bearing witness to the ongoing genocide of the Palestinians.

Comparing it with the Holocaust that took place during World War II, we can see frightening similarities that call for immediate action to stop the genocide. Just like the European Jews were tortured in Nazi Germany's Auschwitz and Dachau, Palestinians are being held in Israeli military prisons that are nothing short of concentration camps, where about 8,000 Palestinians were detained and tortured as of December 2023.[124]

As of the 16th of May 2024, at least 35,173 Palestinians have been killed, and 79,061 have been wounded in Israeli attacks on Gaza since the 7th of October 2023. This genocide is also being called the New Nakba (Catastrophe), marking the immense bloodshed since the 1948 Nakba. More than 550,000 Palestinians

---

[123] Hamburg, D. A. (2015). Preventing Genocide: Practical Steps Toward Early Detection and Effective Action. Routledge.

[124] Euro-Med monitor. (2023). Revealing horrific conditions faced by Palestinian detainees, Euro-Med Monitor calls for immediate international delegation to inspect Israeli detention camps [EN/AR] - occupied Palestinian territory | ReliefWeb. https://reliefweb.int/report/occupied-palestinian-territory/revealing-horrific-conditions-faced-palestinian-detainees-euro-med-monitor-calls-immediate-international-delegation-inspect-israeli-detention-camps-enar

have evacuated Rafah and the north Palestinian territories in the aftermath of the Israeli military's attacks.[125]

The Israel-Palestine conflict has been ongoing since the 1940s, with both sides suffering loss and destruction, but the situation has gained traction and turned into a full-fledged genocide of the Palestinians. The state of Israel has violated international humanitarian law by bombing hospitals, preventing humanitarian aid from reaching the refugees, and bombing predeclared safe zones. For these violations, the established institutions of ICJ and ICC should take notice and intervene. It can only be possible if we unite as a proactive human community and become a factor of change by mobilizing these institutions to take action and stop the genocide.

Despite the efforts of the international community, the Palestinians are still being forced out of their homes, deprived of basic necessities, and bombed even in places that should have been secure for them, such as hospitals and refugee camps. The whole world bears witness to the deadliest and one of the longest genocides in human history, and it is high time that appropriate action is taken to stop it right now and prevent it from happening in the future.

---

[125] Mccready, A., Adler, N., & Quillen, S. (2024). Israel's war on Gaza live: New Nakba as hundreds of thousands flee attacks | Israel War on Gaza News | Al Jazeera. Al Jazeera. https://www.aljazeera.com/news/liveblog/2024/5/15/israels-war-on-gaza-live-new-nakba-as-hundreds-of-thousands-flee-attacks

Conclusion

"It's not enough to say 'never again,' we must act to prevent future atrocities."

- Samantha Power

Genocide is an ancient crime that has magnified with technological advancement and the concept of modernity. In the past, the leading cause of genocide was war and conquest, but now political reasons, hatred toward the other group, and an 'Us vs. Them' mentality have become equally dangerous driving forces for the mass murder of a particular race, ethnicity, social group, etc.

The purpose of writing this book was to educate the readers on the sensitive topic of genocide and to combine all the existing literature on mass atrocities to create a comprehensive guide to genocide and social justice. Social justice can only prevail in both Eastern and Western societies when we start addressing complex topics such as genocide and make an effort to understand the phenomenon to prevent it. We must understand where we stand compared to the past to devise a way forward.

As genocide has repeated throughout history and in some cases like the Palestinian Genocide and the genocides targeting the Rohingya Muslims and the Uyghur Muslims, it shows that the initiatives taken to prevent genocide in the past didn't prove to be successful as it occurred again with increased intensity.

Years of denial and turning a blind eye to genocides while they kept occurring have only strengthened the perpetrators into repeating the heinous crime without the fear of being held accountable and punished for their actions. It is high time that we change the mentality of being silent witnesses and take a proactive approach instead.

Education and awareness are the first steps in addressing a problem and reaching a solution for it. This book serves not only as a comprehensive guide but also as a source of discussion on the multiple points and arguments raised related to genocide. To spark further discussion on preventing genocide, I have proposed two ideas: the Uniform Global Constitution and UN citizenship for refugees. I encourage you, the reader, to debate their feasibility in the current geopolitical climate and come up with further suggestions to promote peace and prosperity for all.

Therefore, I conclude this book with the hope that it serves as a valuable, informative source and encourages people to come up with solutions to mass atrocities and establish world peace.

The path to world peace and social justice is long and arduous. But it is a journey we should embark on together, driven by the conviction that every human life holds inherent value, regardless of race, ethnicity, religion, or social group.

The choice is ours to build a world where difference is celebrated, not weaponized, and where the dignity of every human life is cherished and protected.

www.ingramcontent.com/pod-product-compliance
Lightning Source LLC
LaVergne TN
LVHW010110170826
845678LV00012B/2338